Praise from Corporations

"Stephen's book ***You're Hired – Now What Do You Do?*** and the accompanying online Winning in the Work World information is what all college graduates need before they get to the work world. Coupled with an engaging style and great information Stephen helps excite students on the secrets on becoming ready for the work world."

-James Malinchak
Featured on ABCs Hit TV Show, "Secret Millionaire"
Co-Author, Chicken Soup for the College Soul
Two-Time National College Speaker of the Year
Founder, www.BigMoneySpeaker.com

"Stephen's book, *You're Hired*, is the **perfect guidepost to help young grads start their professional life**. At Cigna, we hire over 100 new people every year. The key message I give them is to develop a *personal brand* that is consistent with their *final destination*. Most young grads will not know their final destination, but making the right decisions along the way is critical."

-John M. Staines
HR Officer, Cigna

"I wish I had a book like this to guide me when I was first starting out. This book is **practical and will open your eyes to the corporate world**."

-Chris Tanco
Executive Vice President of 7-Eleven, Inc

"Being in the search and recruitment business for most of my career, **I encourage every student to read this before they get to the work world!** It will definitely help you stand out and be successful."

-Dhirendra Shantilal
Board Director & Head, Asia Pacific Fircroft Group

"The ninety-day game plan with a checklist at the end of the book gives you a **brilliant guide to know what to do when you enter the work world**. It's practical and is a perfect guide for anyone. Stephen, thank you for sharing your experience."

-Hester Chew
CEO of McDonalds Thailand

"This book highlights the **qualities that most, if not all, employers globally are searching for**. I would certainly recommend it to fresh graduates as well as to educators."

-Mohamed Farouk Hafeez
Senior Executive Vice President,
Human Resources and Management Development,
Americana Group

"Students who invest in preparing for understanding the behavioral aspect of entering the corporate world will have a competitive advantage, and so will companies hiring these graduates. **This well-written book is a must read as it provides tools and methodologies to quickly create necessary skills for students succeeding in the corporate world."**

-Caroline Palmstedt
Talent Management Lead, South East Asia, Monsanto

"It is said that your attitude determines your altitude. Stephen has structured this book in a way you can easily learn ***how*** to build this winning attitude. **Practical, easy to read, with great tips from the Coach's Corner**, this book—especially in chapters 7 and 8 (the written and unwritten rules)—will definitely teach you how to be successful and happy in an organization."

-CK Mohan
Senior Director Human Resources,
Yum Restaurants International

Praise from Students

"I was skeptical at first and wondered if it was just another motivational workshop by a charismatic speaker. But I left feeling so impressed and grateful for the wealth of insightful advice I wished I knew 3 years ago when I was a freshman in university! Then I would definitely spend the next few years honing the skills to better prepare myself for the working world ahead!"

-Tay Soo Han, Singapore Management University

"I would recommend Stephen's G.E.M. training to everyone coming out of college and into the working world. Stephen Krempl helped me realize what skills I needed and told me how to acquire them. **The training was truly insightful."**

-Jesal J. Parekh, Curry College

"Little did I know that this stuff would change my perception of how to become successful and be a powerful force in the business world. Stephen's insights gave me a lot of tools to help me become a more confident, skillful, and insightful person. Stephen was both an inspiring and entertaining presenter, and I would definitely recommend this program to all college students."

-Chelsea Alexandria, Washington State University

"I'm extremely pleased with the results. G.E.M. helped me to forget my fears of public speaking and confidence issues. **Stephen engaged us in such an entertaining way** that got everyone involved. I find myself already working toward growth in a positive direction. I'm so grateful I had the opportunity to attend G.E.M. training. Thank you KCI!"

-Nikita Sahgal, Northeastern University

"This program **is a must for anyone who wishes to change who they are into who they want to be.** Stephen's style is easy-going, enjoyable, and knowledgeable. His sense of humor and personality make the classroom interactions pleasant and relaxed. G.E.M. is an **incredibly useful tool in today's global landscape.**"

-Nghi Nguyen, Esq., Northeastern Alumni

Praise from Educators

" Stephen recently gave presentations to our business students and all the Greek organizations on campus. He was able to easily engage, entertain, and enrich both groups.
We are definitely bringing him back to Milikin."

Dr. J. Mark Munoz
Professor, Management and International Business
Tabor School of Business, Millikin University

"I recommend Stephen and his outstanding G.E.M. workshop. Not only is Stephen an engaging presenter, but also the content on developing executive skills for a globalized corporate world is both relevant and highly effective."

-James Reinnoldt, University of Washington, Lecturer of Managerial Communications and Global Business

"This book and Stephen's material **give students an insider view** of the corporate world. Through techniques like role-play, Stephen's 'playbook' enables students to excel at the workplace. It also provides opportunities to apply best practices and put business theories to use."

-John K. Osiri, Ph.D, Washington State University, College of Business

"I was utterly impressed with Stephen's presentation. His **engaging style** was instrumental in helping students pay attention and participate. I'm confident that if you invite Stephen to your school, you will be pleased with the results."

-Amal Mahmoud, Ph.D, Highline Community College, English as a Second Language Professor

"I have attended two G.E.M. workshops and highly recommend that each and every student attend this great training. I found the tools to be **essential in order to succeed** in the work world after graduation."

-Jaime Barajas, Washington State University, Academic and Retention Counselor

You're Hired... Now What Do You Do?

The College Student's Ultimate Playbook to Learning the Rules and Winning in Any Organization

By Stephen Krempl

You're Hired...Now What Do You Do?
The College Student's Ultimate Playbook to
Learning the Rules and Winning in Any Organization

Published By Krempl Communications International LLC
10 9 8 7 6 5 4 3 2

Global Executive Mindset is a Trademark of Krempl Communications International LLC
1) Self-Improvement 2) Executive Development 3) Leadership Development

Krempl Communications International LLC
Singapore – Singapore Office
38A Circular Rd
Singapore 049394

USA – Issaquah Office
1567 Highlands Dr NE, Suite 110-188
Issaquah, WA 98029

Website: http://www.WinningintheWorkWorld.com

Printed in the United States of America

Dedication

"To the next generation of executives and leaders-students who are doing what others won't so that they will stand out from day one in the highly competitive corporate world."

www.WinningintheWorkWorld.com

Contents

Introduction

Are You Ready For This?

"It's okay to be new at something, but it's better to get a little preparation beforehand. Showing up 'cold' is the worst option."

-Stephen Krempl

When you were young it wasn't all that hard to stand out. It was like tee-ball or youth soccer—everybody got a trophy just for showing up. In high school you had to put in a little more effort to outshine your classmates and get the teacher to notice you. In college, it was a little harder; the classes were larger and there was more competition. However, once you learned the ropes it wasn't so hard to make your mark. Now you've almost graduated again, and you realize that you don't really know what the *real world* has in store. (Yes, some of you have had glimpses of it through internships, but those were controlled environments.) For most of your life, you have understood the actions and intentions of those around you because everyone played in the same "sandbox" and moved up together at the same pace.

But that's all about to change.

Consider your life up to now the "tryouts" for the world after college. And now, you have finished training camp and think you are ready to step into the big leagues with the major players. A small handful can step up "right off the bat" and compete, but most students have a lot to learn to be ready. I'm here to tell you that it's more complicated than you think—and it can eat you alive if you don't come equipped with the right skills. It might be worth spending time thinking about it because you are going to spend several decades in this world.

Have you ever heard of a college football player who got drafted in the first round but just couldn't hack it in the NFL? What about that up-and-coming, star baseball pitcher who got benched after one MLB season? That can happen when you don't know what to expect. You have to be prepared and know what you're getting into, and then your expectations have to meet reality. Remember it is not always the smartest person who gets promoted; more often, it's the one who figures out the rules of the game. I bet someone in college has clued you in on this fact; after all, isn't that why you went to college—to prepare for a career?

If they didn't, don't worry because in this [play]book, I will coach you on how to develop the mindset and skills you need to win. You will discover how different the work world is, learn what to expect, and understand how to act to set yourself apart and get noticed. Perhaps more importantly, because of my experience working for and researching *Fortune 500* companies around the world, **I will give you all of this from the perspective of the employers themselves.**

This book is designed to give you the edge you need to conquer the competition by providing useful tips, commonly asked questions, and insights into key situations you will encounter. It is my goal to shorten the time it takes for you to get up to speed and get noticed in your career regardless of your industry by showing you what to look out for, how to fit in, and how to stand out.

Why I Am The Right Coach

When I first entered the work world, I had already completed two and a half years of military service and was a commission officer. I'd seen a lot, so *naturally* I thought I knew it all. I joined my first organization and was amazed at how dumb all those "old people" were. I started pointing out mistakes the company was making (and many times I was right), but I soon began to find that the people in my organization didn't like it when some rookie pointed out all their mistakes and suggested the way I thought things should be without them being asked. It felt like I was constantly banging my head against the wall, and after four years, I concluded that I was an utter failure. But I shook it off, discovered what I really wanted to do, and I went back to school.

That's when I realized what college was NOT teaching. Much of what I learned in college to prepare for the real world was incomplete at best. I was grateful for what I did learn, especially from my professors, but because of what I had experienced before I returned to school, I found that the most essential skills for success in the work world were missing from the college experience. Through a lot of trial and error and a lot of time, I figured out the missing ingredients for making my mark and went on to have standout careers at Motorola, PepsiCo, Yum! Brands and Starbucks.

> Consider your life up to now the tryouts for the world after college.

After years of working with top executives at these major corporations, I decided to start my own company and began teaching a program called **Global Executive Mindset (G.E.M.)** that is designed to help future leaders with high potential get noticed. After conducting endless research for this program and getting great results, I realized that even top executives with years of experience were never given a framework to stand out in their organizations. *How could this be?* When I was in college it seemed glaringly obvious to me what elements were missing, and without even realizing it I had been practicing those skills all along that moved me ahead and got me noticed over my competition.

That got me thinking. Wouldn't it be great if the future workforce learned those skills and practiced them before they got to the work world? So I started teaching those skills to college students. I want to make sure you understand how the professional world truly operates, which is why it is my mission is ***"to help every student figure out what is expected of them and learn those behaviors before they enter the work world."***

Why You Need This Playbook

As a student entering the work world, it's never been so hard to stand out. It used to be that a strong work ethic got you everywhere. But things have changed. Today, it's all about Being Ready, Being Confident, Being Noticed and Being Promotable. **But HOW do you do all this?** In a technology driven world, you have to balance texting, talking, positioning, and posting *everything* on Facebook, Instagram, and Twitter with knowing what you can say about your company, your colleagues, and your superiors (and their secrets) and what you can't.

School is an important foundation, but it is just that—the *foundation* for something more substantial. There's a lot more to learn. The competition for jobs is increasingly cutthroat, not to mention it has become a worldwide competition, as companies are searching for talent across the globe. You need a way to STAND OUT and shorten your learning curve—**and that's why you need this book.** School taught you what you need to know. Now I will tell you *what to do* with that knowledge and *how to understand the rules of the game and how to communicate* what you know in your new environment.

Here's the Game Plan

This is more than a book, it's your homerun bat, it's your lucky game ball, and it's your playbook for the upcoming game. We will cover the key insights and skills that will get you on the fast track and allow you to make fewer errors (you still have to make some—we all do in order to learn and become skilled at our crafts). You want to make an impact, get promoted, make more money, and stand out. With powerful tips and information, researched and tested in the real world by real people, this book is filled with practical ideas that you can implement immediately to get you closer to your goals and dreams—and get you there faster.

You will find situations, examples and scenarios that you will encounter in the work world that will answer critical questions like: Do you speak up first or wait until the end at an important meeting? What do you say when you're in the elevator with your boss, a colleague you don't know, or your CEO? How do you make an impression in a room with a hundred people or more? What do you do if someone else asks the same question you were about to ask?

I will help you determine the best emotional, intellectual and behavioral skill sets for your career, and then I will provide you with the framework to **navigate the organization**, **identify specific cultural rules** for your organization, **communicate confidently**, **connect personally** and **stand out** in the corporate world. By the time you reach the end, you will be more aware of critical elements in the workplace and have the chance to practice things you may not have even realized mattered. The goal is to sound more poised and more prepared than the person who joined the team at the same time you did.

> School taught you what you need to know. So how can you now communicate what you know in your new environment?

This book will give you an exclusive peek behind the locker room door (the office), as well as a tour of the stadium (the industry) and the training facilities (the company) before the other teams (the competition) come out to play on game day. Even if you are a rookie, you want others to feel like you've played the game before. You have to act like you know what you're doing, or even better, actually *know* what you're doing! You have to look ready. And you have to sound ready. You have to be ready.

It's your choice—you can either bang your head against a wall like I did for the first few years, or you can do some pre-game preparation and warm-up. Today, your work doesn't always speak for itself. **<u>You</u>** have to understand the expectations required of you so that you can speak up more confidently and learn how to get prepared, add value, be different and be proactive. Don't get frustrated trying to figure it all out. Let me help you shortcut the first few months or years by learning the things you didn't hear in school.

ARE YOU READY FOR THIS?

IT'S TIME TO GET YOUR GAME FACE ON.

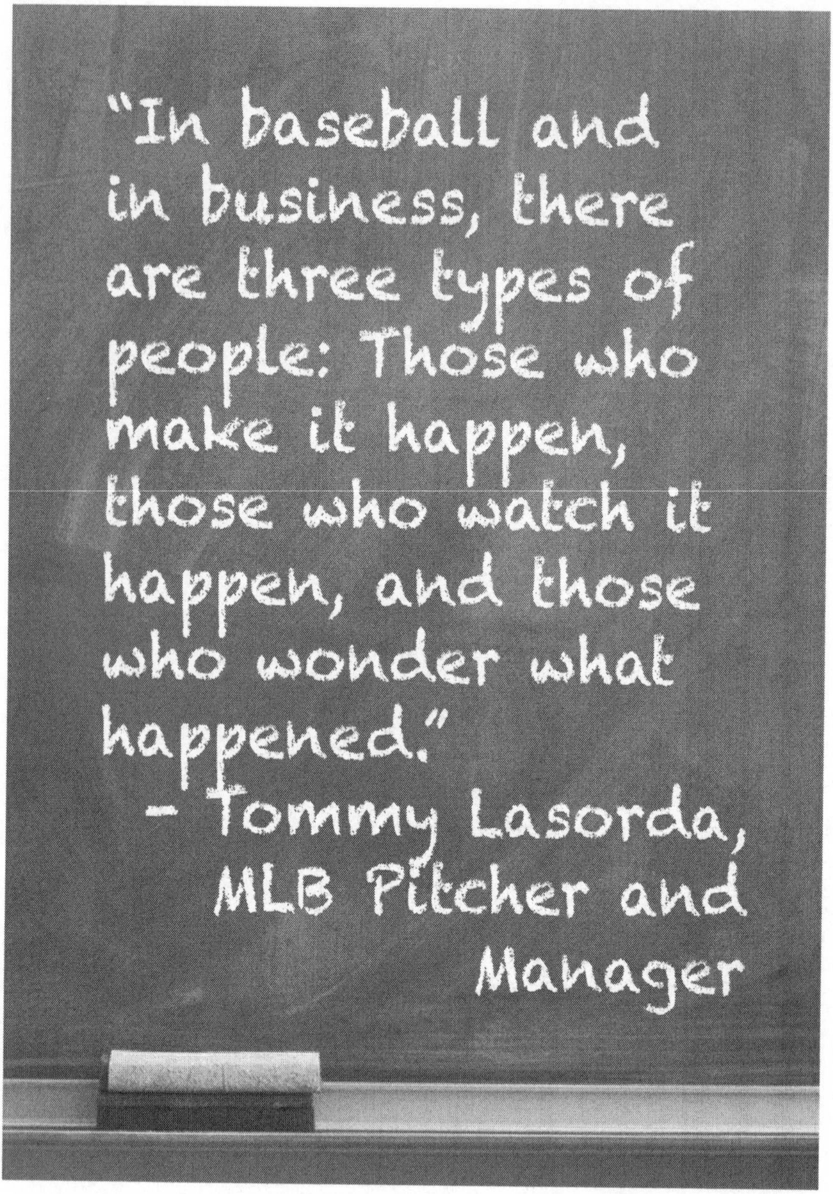
"In baseball and in business, there are three types of people: Those who make it happen, those who watch it happen, and those who wonder what happened."
- Tommy Lasorda, MLB Pitcher and Manager

Chapter 1

The Work World: What's Different and How to Get Ready For It

> *"School was great, but it was preparing you for something bigger. Now you are there—and I hope you are prepared."*
>
> -Stephen Krempl

Sports are, by their very nature, competitive. The whole point—after all—is to win. There are SCORES at the end of the game so that everyone knows who was the best and who lost. Players have published STATS that tell the world how they did. Recruiters and talent SCOUTS are continually searching for the right players who can enhance the team's strengths or plug their weaknesses. When players get drafted, the COACHES are there to take and mold them to be their best so the team can win the big Championship TROPHY at the end of the season. Once the season is over, they do it all over again—proving themselves, getting ahead, and hopefully staying there.

There are many TEAM ROLES to fill on a well-functioning team. Players know it's critical for them to understand their roles and contribute if they want to keep playing. There may be only one STAR quarterback, pitcher or center forward, but the best teams know that everyone in their organization plays an integral part—from the grounds keepers to the assistant coaches—that enables the team to operate like a well-oiled machine. COMPETITION is fierce, and coaches know that they have to stay ahead and keep opponents guessing. They also know that CHANGE is constant and essential; and being predictable can be the kiss of death.

Key Parallels of Sports and Work

That is the sports world in a nutshell. Why does all of this matter to you, right here and right now? Well, some say that we never leave behind the politics and hierarchies established in high school (jocks and head cheerleaders, cliques, and inner circles); and the same can be said for our inherent desire to win. It's embedded in us and in our culture. The need for competition and the race to get ahead will always be there—and this is especially true in the corporate world. It can be cutthroat and relentless, and if you don't stay sharp, it will make you obsolete before you've had your morning coffee. Every company has a different style through which they operate, and you must be prepared for them all.

In the world of business, it looks a little different (there's no scoreboard or stadium) but it's essentially the same. The SCORES are there—Wall Street keeps track of your team's STATS, and so does your boss. He has his own kind of scorecards, performance targets, and bonus objectives. Companies send out talent SCOUTS who search for the best talent who fit into the culture and the open positions. Companies may even try to steal key players from other companies in order to bring their skills to the organization. Managers and senior staff act as COACHES to help train you in your new role. And the entire company is working toward the Championship TROPHY at the end of the year, which could be outranking the competition, delivering record earnings to shareholders, giving bonuses, or going public through an IPO.

Just as in the world of sports, every TEAM ROLE in the company serves its purpose for the greater good of the organization. There may only be one STAR CEO, but the best companies know that everyone in their organization—from the receptionist to the warehouse manager to the sales team—has to be on the same page in order to edge out the COMPETITON. And of course, CHANGE is constant and essential; and everyone is required to learn and grow or risk becoming irrelevant. And of course, the ultimate key is that customer in the marketplace who is willing to buy your product or service.

Your customers have a choice, and if you don't perform to their expectations, they will take their business elsewhere. And that is where the sports world has an advantage over the business world. In sports, the die-hard fans will support the team through thick and thin (most of the time). But many customers aren't so patriotic—if they expect one experience only to have a less pleasant one, they will abandon your side of the bleachers.

> Before you begin your career, decide NOW whether you will contribute to the bottom line or detract from it.

So your job is to help the company keep and grow its customer base and its business. You have to ask yourself if you are contributing to customer loyalty or detracting from it. Adopt this thought process early and you will go far in your career. Too many people start off their careers with the feeling that the company owes them a living. These types of employees will never be true contributors to the team. If you don't learn to believe in the plays and follow them, how is your team going to win?

You don't have to be drafted in the first round (or go to the best school or have the best GPA) to be successful. You can start from the bottom and work your way up. Some just do it faster than others, but that probably had little to do with the grades on their transcripts. No matter where you come from, you have strengths that your supervisor needs to know about and utilize. We are going to discover how to reveal those strengths in the most impactful way.

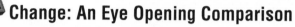

Change: An Eye Opening Comparison

Change is constant. The sports world knows it—and successful businesses definitely know it. But do you know it? More importantly, do you embrace it? We've established some similarities to sports and the work world, and you were probably even able to relate some of the concepts to your college experience. But there are some distinct changes that occur during your leap from college to the work world that must be addressed. After all, effectively managing expectations is what makes real change possible. Take a closer look at the table on the next page for some important disparities between school and work.

This chart is intended to give you a glimpse into the vast differences awaiting you outside the boundaries of your cozy campus. Maybe you've decided to work for a large corporation after you graduate; or perhaps you have always wanted to become an entrepreneur and "be your own boss." It doesn't matter whether you work for yourself or someone else, everything in the chart applies to your future. In fact, if you work for yourself, be prepared to have longer hours and fewer vacation days. Things changed from high school to college; but those were minor changes—and now we're talking about the major league changes. So let's figure out how to be ready.

The Most Important Question

We've compared sports and work. We've compared college and work. But before we take our analogies and comparisons any further, I need to ask you an important question, perhaps the most important question you've ever been asked. Let's say you are planning to work for a large corporation, and

Categories	School	Work
Hours	Classes 3-4 times a week + study time = 20-30 hrs a week (4 hours in class)	Work 8+ hours a day + overtime + work at home = 40-60 hrs a week (40+ hours in office)
Semesters	Classes last 12-16 weeks. They end and new ones begin.	Assignments for weeks, months, years. Won't end until you switch company or roles.
Teams	You choose your friends.	You can't choose your colleagues.
Functions	Choose your major after 2 years	Belong to a department from day 1
Vacation	Summer break, Mid-term breaks, Winter break, snow days, homecoming, etc.	10-14 vacation days. Might get a few sick days (possibly paid).
Seniority	Promoted from freshmen to senior as you meet credit/major requirements.	Promotions not guaranteed (based on performance, etc). May report to younger supervisor in the future.
Professors	Several per semester, all give a different grade. See them a few times a week.	One supervisor gives your performance appraisal. You likely see this person everyday.
Participation	Optional—in large classes, you can tune out without consequence.	Required—if you don't participate in meetings, you'll look like an idiot.
Extra Credit	Opportunity to make up for missed lessons or assignments.	No extra credit for botched work or missed deadlines.

you are ready for a great company to instantly recognize your awesomeness and snatch you up. You were a regular at the career center, you got your resume professionally done, and you interviewed well and got hired. Congratulations! Now here is the question:

Now what do you do next that will best prepare you for this opportunity?

It's your first day at your new job. You're ready to take on the world. You think you are prepared. But are you? Are you planning to act like you did at college? Can you drop an assignment the same way you dropped a class because you didn't like the professor? Remember how some students (not you of course) were always late to class, didn't prepare for lectures, refused to participate, looked bored all the time, and posted "selfies" to Instagram during lessons? They got away with it, right? Do you think you'll get away with any of this at your new job?

As strange as it sounds, there is not much about college life that prepares you for work life. Did you take any classes that taught the proper behavior for day one, week one, or month one in the real world? No. They expected you to just magically figure it out. Well, consider this a crash course in Real World 101.

Let's pretend you landed a job at your top company of choice, which is Boeing. It's your first day, and you walk in to meet your supervisor. He says, "Hi Tom, good morning and welcome aboard. Tell me a little about yourself and why you chose Boeing."

> There is no room in the major leagues for players who aren't prepared.

You begin your reply with, "Well, uh…" Then you start talking to yourself: *Wait a minute, what do I say??? Does it matter? What's the right answer? What's the wrong answer? Is he expecting something specific?* Inside you start to panic. Fear spreads across your face. Your hands get cold and clammy. In short, you instantly look like you're way out of your league.

That's a problem. There is no room for "uh" in the real world (for those who expect their careers to go places). The only reason someone says "Uh…" is because he or she wasn't expecting that question or doesn't have a good answer. This is a bad idea—and it makes an even worse first impression. That is why you need to ensure you are prepared for this and many other questions before you ever hear them. Don't allow your first meeting with key personnel to be the first time you've thought about important questions.

The only way you're going to appear confident and make any kind of lasting impression is to think through your response to questions like, "Tell me a little about yourself and why you choose this company." Let's go back to the scenario where you are working for Boeing. Here is a better response to that question:

"Stephen, first of all, thank you for giving me the opportunity to be on your team. There are three key things that I hope to be able to contribute: 1) My extensive knowledge of the latest innovative satellite technology 2) My ability to skillfully complete rapid prototyping with 3D data and 3) My willingness to stay teachable and learn from the resident experts in the industry.

And since I have researched the company extensively, I know I will enjoy working for a company who: 1) Leverages their global strengths 2) Fosters a collaborative workspace and 3) Places an emphasis on large-scale systems integration, which was the focus of my senior project. Thanks for the opportunity to learn from the team."

Impressive right? I bet the supervisor thought so, too. Do you think many other newcomers walk in with a response like that? So what does that mean for you? It means you'll stand out from day one. Obviously your responses will vary depending on your skill set and the company itself, but regardless of what you bring to the table or where you work, you need to have at least a rough idea of what to say instead of making stuff up on the fly. I know some people are good at improvisation, but when it comes to your future, don't leave anything to chance. A little preparation goes a long way.

Coach's Corner

Start Practicing Like a Professional

"More sweat in training; less blood in battle."

-Peter Hearl

It has been said that, "There is no glory in practice, but without practice, there is no glory." Pro athletes become pro athletes because they practiced their talents day-in and day-out throughout their lives, even when no one was watching (and especially when no one was watching). And that's what you need to do in order to get to the level you want to reach.

So, now I want you to answer the previous question from the chapter for yourself and your situation. If you already have your first job or know where you plan to work, that will the basis for your answer. If you have not yet gotten your first job, then you can practice using your "dream" company or the place where you had an internship or worked at in college. Then you can use this as a template for your first day:

Tell me a little about yourself and why you choose this company:

a) First of all, thank you [____________________] for giving me the opportunity to be on your team. There are three key things that I can contribute to the team:

1. ____

2. ____

3. ____

And since I have researched our company, I know I will enjoy working for one that:

1. ______________________________

2. ______________________________

3. ______________________________

Thanks for the opportunity to learn from the team.

You could also start with:

My name is ____________ I majored in ____________ at ____________ University, (Then continue with (a) from above.)

After you determine what you are going to say during the first few minutes in the first meeting, in a small group, or in orientation class, that is not enough. You must then practice it. As you have no doubt heard many times before (but perhaps never internalized), practice does make perfect. If you'd like to use my interactive online program that allows you to rehearse live and then play it back to see how you sound, go to my website: www.stephenkrempl.com/practice or download the app.

I guarantee that your competition (the other people who want your job and other competing companies) will try every trick in the book to outshine you. So, why not use every tool at your disposal to become your absolute best?

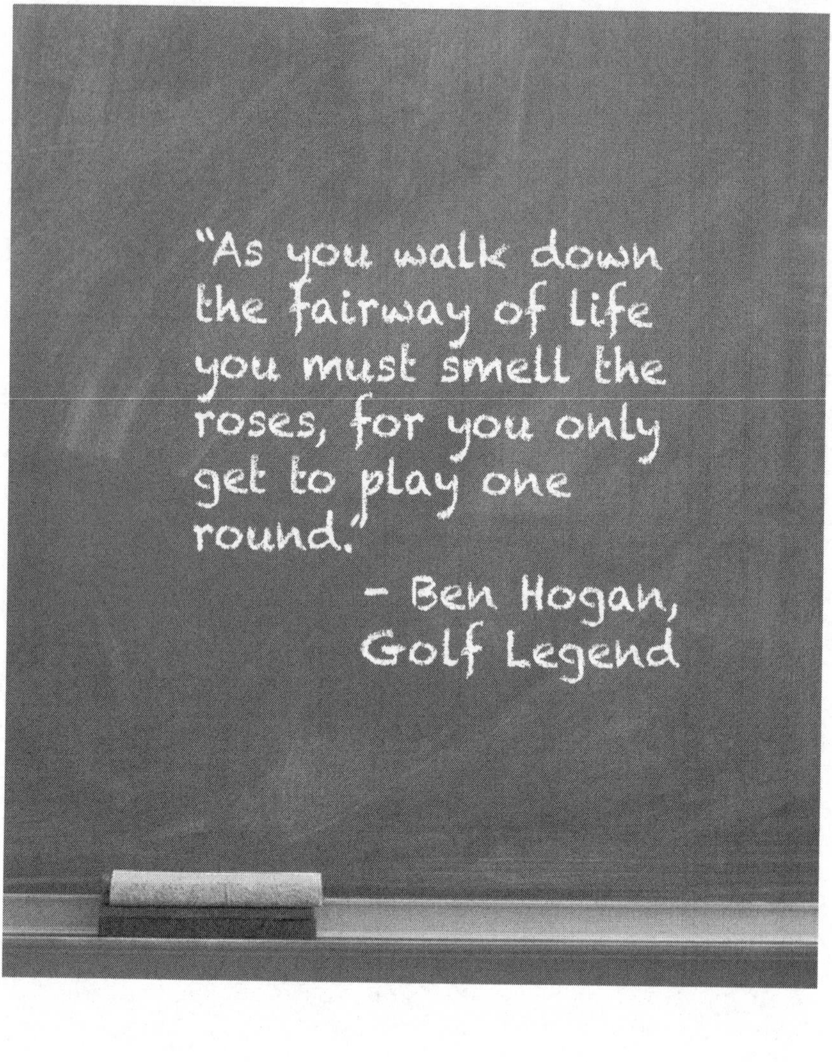
"As you walk down
the fairway of life
you must smell the
roses, for you only
get to play one
round."
- Ben Hogan,
Golf Legend

Chapter 2

Your Game Plan: Rules to Build Your Career By

"It's the big leagues, and there is always someone in line right behind you ready to take your spot on the roster. Be someone who gets remembered."
-Stephen Krempl

When a player joins his professional team for the first time on the field, there are probably a lot of thoughts racing through his or her mind. They may range from "*I'm in way over my head*" all the way to "*I was born to be here.*" Whatever you are thinking, know that those first few moments on the field are critical to proving to your coaches, teammates, and fans that you belong.

You have the same chance to prove yourself as you begin your new career; and as you progress through this book, my hope is that you don't view it as work, but rather as a unique opportunity. You have ***one shot*** to make the kind of first impression you want to make, and because you chose to read this playbook, you are one of the few who are privileged enough to know how to prepare for those critical career moments. *You are taking control of your own destiny and calling your own shots.*

Like it or not, you will be always compared to the next person or latest member of the team. It's up to you to have the comparison weigh in your favor. So, how do you stand out in any size organization, especially when you're the new kid on the block? The keys are confidence, communication, and connection—and throughout this book, you will gain insight into each of these three areas. There are also some lesser-known skills for getting noticed and making an impact. I call them the ***Three Skills for Becoming an MVP***, and they are your tickets to staying off the sidelines and in the game.

MVP Skill #1: Become a Problem Solver

The first one may sound like a no-brainer, but it is not quite as simple as it sounds. If you can truly solve the problems—I repeat—if you can *truly* solve the problems of your company, bosses, supervisors, colleagues or friends, then you will get ahead and stay there. How do you solve someone else's problems? Let me tell you a story:

When I went to college, the first class I took my freshman year was OB321. Of course, we all know you're not supposed to take a 300 level class during the first semester of your freshman year. But I was already twenty-five. I had worked for four years. I thought I knew a thing or two about Organizational Behavior.

On the first day of class, everyone shuffled in and sat down. When I walked in, I went right up and introduced myself to the professor. "Hi, my name is Stephen Krempl. I'm from Singapore. Professor Graham, is there anything I can do for you?"

He looked genuinely surprised and replied, "That is interesting. I'm going to Singapore to present a keynote at a worldwide conference." (That was a fortunate and unexpected coincidence.)

My wheels started turning. "Conference? What are you speaking about?"

"I'm going to talk about Intercultural Team Effectiveness."

That was not really my area of expertise, but I said, "If you give me a couple of hours in the TV studio, I'll cut a short video for you. I'll script it and get the actors together. I'll give it to you, and if you use it in your conference, you'll be a star."

He looked stunned. "You can do that?"

I smiled. "Yup."

Do you think I knew exactly what I was going to do at that moment? Definitely not. But I had done videos before, and if I did one for this professor, I may be able to solve his problem. Did any other student offer to help him? They were all just sitting there, staring at the back of someone else's head. So I was determined to do whatever it took to make the video, which I did. I knew a lot about Singapore, and I researched the rest until I found the content for a script that would appeal to the audience. He played it at his conference, and he was, in fact, a hit.

What did that do for me? A few weeks into his class, I guaranteed my 'A.' I still had to take the exams and do the work, but because I solved a problem for that professor, I jumped to the top of the short list of his favorite and most remembered students. I recognized that someone had a problem. Professor Graham was going to a place where he had no background experience, and it just so happened that I had the right background to help him. I did a little bit of research, wrote a script, cut a video, and solved his problem.

> Solve a problem for your boss and you'll solidify your place as an all-star on the team.

When you arrive at your new company, start looking for ways to help or problems to solve. Then, once you recognize an issue or problem, you must ask yourself:• Department or company's biggest problem and can I help solve it?

- What from my background can I leverage or how can I find the information to help?
- How can I be of value and contribute?

These questions are critical, because if you tell someone you can help them and then you don't or can't, that is sometimes worse than not trying at all.

When I joined Motorola years ago, I became the final member of a group with nine total members, including Don, our supervisor. Our team was an instructional design group that was tasked to redesign training programs for the Singapore government. When I started, I worked hard to learn the lay of the land so I could fully understand how things worked and how to meet our deadlines for the project. I noticed that Don was concerned that seed funding for the project was about to end and he needed to find ways to raise revenue. Because I had immersed myself in the inner workings of the department and the company I had already discovered a few possible ways to achieve that.

I decided to write Don an email about my thoughts on the situation. I was not sure how he would react, but I went ahead with my suggestion. The email read:

> *"Don, I think we have an opportunity to leverage our company's name and our six sigma quality expertise. Here is my suggestion for how we can use that to increase revenue and build a new business segment..."*

I explained the idea in detail and hit send. Within an hour Don popped his head in my cubicle and said, "Hey Steve, come into my office." When I got there, he sat me down, and said, "So, do you think your idea will work?"

What do you think my response was? "YES, I THINK IT CAN WORK." I wasn't sure it would work, not 100 percent sure at least. No one is ever completely sure when it comes to business decisions that involve selling a new product, but what mattered is that I saw a problem and addressed it. I was the only team member who even attempted to offer a solution; and when the time came for a promotion from within our team, whose name do you think was at the top of the list? It was the guy who had a good idea for how to increase revenue and was bold enough to share it.

MVP Skill #2: Be Interested (and Pay Attention)

Most people don't listen. *People simply wait.* They wait for their turn to speak. And what do these "waiters" do while you're talking? They are rehearsing in their head what they are going to say instead of paying attention to the person who is speaking. What they should be doing is listening and formulating a response that will make them sound better and stand out.

What can you do about this? Join in the madness and contribute to chronic miscommunication? Here is what you should do: First of all (and this is so simple that it still shocks me how few people do it), don't wait your turn—pay attention and listen! When you stop and listen, you differentiate yourself from all your other co-workers who are biding their time until you shut your mouth so they can open theirs.

If you really want to stand out, don't be a "me too" kind of person—a colleague who always agrees with everyone else's point of view. When someone shares his or her view on something, don't just say, " I agree." Take the extra step by saying, "I agree with Tom, and my take on this is…" By doing this, you will add value to the discussion. Of course, you don't have to say something if you don't have anything substantive to add, but you still have to pay attention to what's going on instead of reading your text messages or email. Otherwise, you may miss a real opportunity to stand out, or worse, someone may call on you, and your only response will be, "Err, sorry. What was that again?"

> If you want to stand out, then shut up and listen.

MVP Skill #3: Keep Your Career off Autopilot (and Focus on Being GREAT!)

In sports, how do the washed-up players and the has-been's end up on the bench? Many times, it's because they didn't stay sharp. They didn't stay current. And the next guy waiting to take the spotlight passed right by them. There will be moments in your career when it may be tempting to go on "auto pilot" and work just enough not to get fired. A few professional players—and many of the people you will meet throughout your career—start thinking that their talents will carry them without putting in the extra work. That is why the third and final skill for becoming an MVP in your organization is a wake up call:

You're only as good as the person who comes before you and the person who comes after you.

Your actions and ideas from yesterday's meeting are important, and so is that project last month that received accolades from your superiors in the company. But the only things that matter today are your current activities and contributions. Look, I already know you are good. You're at a good school. You're probably in a good major. You're good or want to get good—otherwise you wouldn't even be reading this.

But I don't want you to be good. I want you to be great! Jim Collins wrote a book called *Good to Great*, and no one could say it any better. That's what you want for your career—not just good performance, but greatness. You don't want someone to describe you like this, "Julie performs her job pretty well and is usually on time." You want people to say, "Boy, she is one sharp individual! Watch out for Julie. We're all going to be working for her one day."

Are you starting to understand the level that your performance needs to reach in the corporate world? And we've barely even scratched the surface! The best news is that you don't have to incorporate everything you read in this book. In fact, two or three things can make all the difference. Now, you may be shaking your head with doubt right now and thinking, "You don't understand, Stephen. I'm different. I'm not the kind of person who can single himself out in a crowd. I'm just not wired that way. I'll have to stand out in my own quiet way." Or "You don't understand Stephen. I don't have this… I don't have that…" Those aren't reasons. *Those are excuses.*

Those types of responses represent a problem with attitude and a tendency to shirk responsibility or it stems from plain mediocrity. Maybe you've never really taken responsibility for anything in your life. If that's you, you are certainly not alone. Modern society perpetuates the *victim's mentality*. But let me ask you this—do you think your boss will care about your excuses or appreciate the fact that you only take ownership of a decision when it was successful? Do you think you can say, "You don't understand, Boss. I worked really hard but…?" Your boss won't hear your excuses (or whining), no matter how valid you think they are. All he or she will hear is, "I didn't get it done." But all your boss really wants to hear is, "I solved the problem."

Make a Decision to be GREAT

Greatness—it's a decision you have to make, and then you have to re-make it every single morning. Some might argue that there's nothing wrong with being good, but Jim Collins writes that the enemy of *great* is *good*. When you start believing your "good" is enough, you're in trouble. You're only as good as the person who comes before you or comes after you—and you don't want to be good; you want to be *great*.

Are you ready to be Great?

I know what it's like to want to hide behind an excuse. We all have things in our past that can hold us back if we let them. *I know*. Our family didn't have much money when I was growing up. I could have easily said, "You don't understand. I come from a poor background." I could have somehow justified why I didn't want to put in the effort to contribute or to win. It's safer to assume that people just don't "get you" and then put up a wall that you never emerge from. But the *safest* way is usually also the way to mediocrity and regret.

Whenever I deliver my programs, a student will come up to me afterwards and start the conversation with, "But Stephen you don't understand..." My response to whatever excuse follows is, "Okay. And your point is?" No one is interested in *why you can't.* In the business world, they want to know *how you will.* And the higher you climb, the greater this expectation becomes.

Have you ever been to a career fair? Those places can be mad houses, and I often hear students say that they are a waste of time. I assume you went there to meet recruiters and people from companies where you might work, right? Before you went, did you write down exactly what you were going to say at each introduction? Then did you rehearse the intro over and over again? And did you prepare a couple of great questions so that the representatives from these companies would remember you? If you didn't do that, then no wonder you thought it was a waste of time (and you became a waste of the recruiters' time as well).

The next time you visit a career fair, try this: ***Prepare***. And I'm not just talking about having plenty of copies of your resume and wearing a nice suit. Practice your intro until you internalize it, and then practice it again with an energetic approach, armed with information on the company. You know you aren't the only person there. (Duh.) So figure out what differentiates you—we all have something—and use that in your intro!

> No one is interested in why you can't. They want to know how you will.

Meeting professionals in the real world isn't like meeting the members of your fraternity or your classmates. ***The people you meet in the business world are ready to forget you the moment they shake your hand.*** It's the big leagues, and there is someone in line right behind you ready to take your spot on the roster. You

Coach's Corner

Determine Your Purpose and Direction

don't have to be the "star" player, but you can certainly become an important and indispensable part of the team.

Time to answer a few tough questions. Maybe this is the first time you've really been honest with yourself, so take your time and think about your responses, and then jot down your best answers:

Why are you at college?

____

____

What do your professors want from you?

____

____

What are you hoping to get from your classes?

____

____

Now, here are those questions again, but worded for your new life outside college:

Why are you at work?

____

____

____

What do your employers want from you?

____

____

What are you hoping to get from your job?

____

____

____

If you do not have these questions answered before you sit down at your desk on the first day, you are making a mistake that you may regret for the rest of your professional career. When you know the "why" behind your job, it will be easier to spot opportunities to stand out, no matter where you start your career. Everyone falls into a functional area; but you may start as the ball girl or water boy and end up being the coach. Some make it to coach at age thirty others at age fifty. *What kind of career do you want to have?* Here are a few more questions to ask yourself as you practice for your new career and new life in the big leagues:

Why did I take this job?

____

____

____

What do I want to achieve?

____

____

____

How do I want to leverage this opportunity? What am I prepared to do?

____

____

I wish someone had shared these insights with me when I was starting out in corporate America. I had no idea what I was doing. I got hired, I walked in, and that was about as far as I had planned. I basically told my superiors, "You guys are idiots." (I said it a little differently than that, but that was the message I conveyed.) Do you think anyone appreciated my intelligent insights given my delivery method? No they did not. In fact, I'm amazed I didn't get fired before I wised up.

You can only pretend you know what you're doing for so long, so the more opportunities you get to practice and find out what to expect, the better off you'll be. In essence, you want to avoid those "deer in the headlights" moments as much as you can. If you are a junior or senior, your time to prepare is NOW, and if you are a freshmen or sophomore, hallelujah! You've got a few more years to practice.

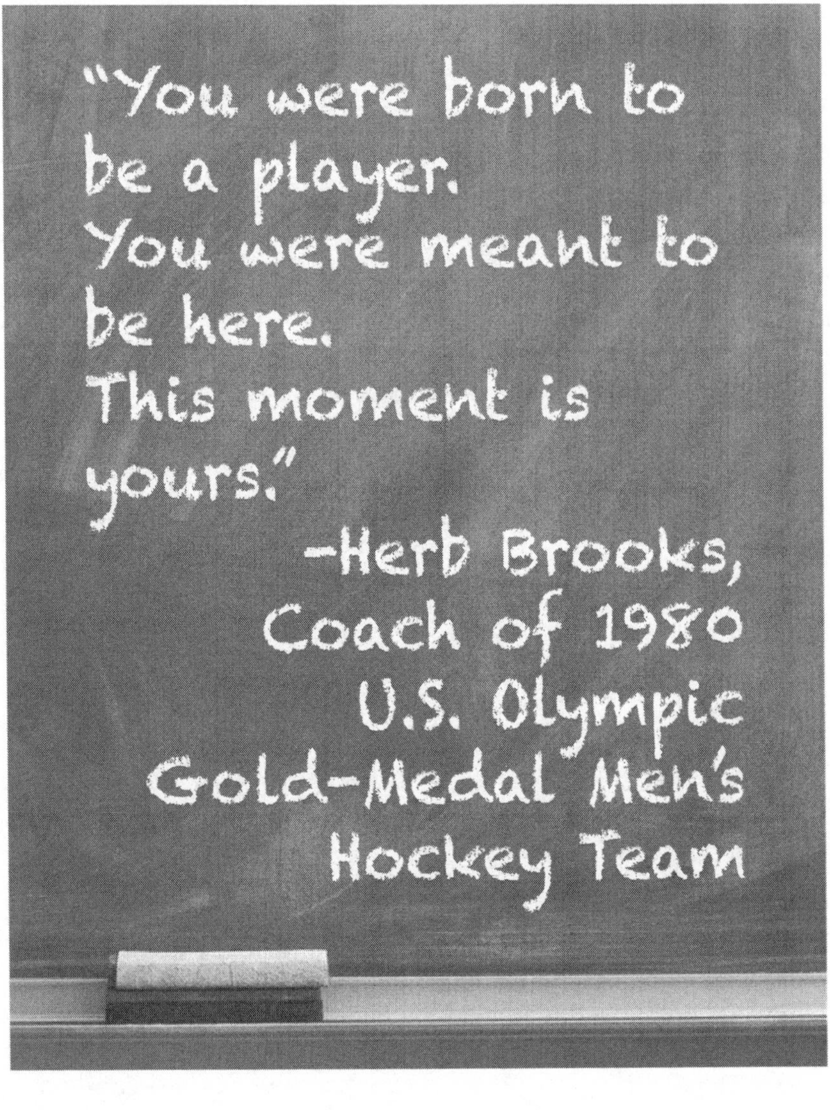
"You were born to
be a player.
You were meant to
be here.
This moment is
yours."
-Herb Brooks,
Coach of 1980
U.S. Olympic
Gold-Medal Men's
Hockey Team

Chapter 3

Choose Your Game: Which Career Path is Best for You?

"It DOES matter what your resume says. It's the first impression that all future employers will have of you, so it's up to you to make sure it's a good one."

-Stephen Krempl

Most professional athletes play the game they play because it's where their passions lie. It's the game or sport they grew up playing. It's what they've been dreaming about their entire lives. The accountant in the cubicle next to yours or the salesperson on the twenty-seventh work related trip of the year probably didn't grow up dreaming about his or her current position. In fact, most of us don't end up becoming what we think we want to be when we grow up. If we did, we'd all be doctors, firefighters, or astronauts. (But if you are in your dream job, then good on you!)

However your reality stacks up to your expectations, it doesn't mean you can't thoroughly enjoy your work or derive extreme satisfaction from what you do—in fact, it's critical that you enjoy or get satisfaction from your work. It simply means that you have to be careful as you select your major in college. This chapter is all setting yourself up for a successful journey by carefully choosing the game you want to play.

A Tough Decision

It's graduation day, a day you've probably dreamed about for years. It's the day when the world officially recognizes you as an "adult" who is ready to enter the real world—where all the pros play. It should be the most exciting time of your life, but there's one small thing bothering you. (Well, maybe it's not such a small thing.) You picked a major based on what you think you like or what others have told you that you're good at; but now that it's crunch time, is it really what you want to do?

> You have to pick the game you want to play and then decide to be the best (no matter what major you choose).

How do you pick the industry and profession—the game you want to play—that will be your focus for years to come? It's a huge decision. In fact, it's one of the hardest parts about this time of life; and if you find yourself unsure where to work or even what to do, you certainly aren't alone. Most graduates feel this way at some point during college or during the first few years after school. They finish school, only to find themselves asking, "How can I *really* know where I want to work or what position will suit me best?" In college, you may have gotten away with vacillating back and forth for a few years between majors. But now that you are about to enter the "major league" playing field, you just can't do that anymore. You have to pick the game you want to play—and then master it. If you want to be a professional athlete, do you think you'd try to get recruited for tennis, golf, basketball *and* hockey? That just isn't how it's done. You pick one sport and become the best that you can be at it. Sure, there are athletes who excel at many sports, but the best athletes in the world are known for ONE and only one sport.

So what does that mean for you? It means that "career hopping" won't land you on the fast track to success. It does not mean you can't do it to figure out what you really like, but I suggest you do it within the first 3 years. The fact is that if you make a "career" out of career hopping, it will derail you and your future. Let's examine why this tends to be the case. Pretend you are a corporate recruiter, and you have been tasked to fill a new HR position at a *Fortune 100* firm. Today you are meeting with two candidates. Here is how the conversation starts with **Candidate #1, named Andrea**:

> "Yeah, so I've been in the work world for fi ve years now. In college I was a business major with a concentration in Accounting. I thought I would like that, but it didn't really fi tme. So I worked in the Marketing Department for two years.Man, those marketing people were so obnoxious! Th at's howI ended up in Human Resources as a generalist for two years.It's not really my favorite, but I am still fi guring out if it's a good place for me. Only time will tell, I guess!"

As a recruiter, what are your impressions of Andrea? Chances are Andrea's resume probably looks about as scattered as her conversation sounds. Now let's hear what **Candidate #2, named Teddy,** has to say:

> "As a Business major with an emphasis in Human Resources, I was determined to get into an HR role. So I started in the Compensation and Benefits Department for two years, and then I moved over to Employee Relations to deal with union issues for the next two years. Then I accepted my current role as HR Generalist supporting the business unit, where I've been for the past year."

At first blush, Teddy has also held several different roles over the first five years of his career. But what was the major difference? That's right—all of Teddy's positions were within the SAME department. He concentrated on HR and decided to make it stick. His resume signifies that he is not a "flight risk" and is worth the time and investment it takes to train a new team member.

As much as we like to think that we speak for ourselves, and that once we get our foot in the door our resume doesn't really matter, this just isn't the truth. It DOES matter what your resume says. It's the first impression that all future employers will have of you, so it's up to you to make sure it's a good one.

The [Internship] Path to Success

If you have ever been to the career center at your school, chances are you have taken at least one career or personality assessment like the *Strong-Campbell Interest Inventory*, the *Myers-Briggs Type Indicator*, or the *Keirsey Temperament Sorter*, among others. For those of you haven't taken a survey or maybe it's been a while, let me remind you. Career assessment surveys assess your personality and interests to determine what careers might best suit you. If you have taken a survey, that is great. But it's only the first step. There's a lot more to do before you graduate and pursue whatever career you may think you're best suited for.

Let's say you took a survey when you first came to school as a freshman. Here is a possible plan of action during the course of your college career:

YEAR ONE. Take a survey. Based on the inventory, identify the two or three career paths you may want to pursue. If are already confident that you want be a doctor or engineer, for example, then you must also choose what type or specialty you want to practice. Then during the course of your freshman year, identify the possible industries and specific companies you could work for in each of your two or three potential career choices.

YEAR TWO. Talk to one of the top companies you want to work for. Find out more about them and get an internship in that company. If that company is not located near your college or your town, get an internship at a similar company.

YEAR THREE. Repeat the steps from year two, except this time, intern for another company (possibly in another industry).

YEAR FOUR. Repeat the steps from year three, or possibly re-intern at one of the companies from year two or three if you found a company you like.

Despite the commonly held belief, internships are not just a "senior year thing." Many students try to cram all of this real-world activity into their last year (or even their final semester), but by then, it merely becomes a frantic race to beat the clock and pick out what you want to do before you graduate. The top students start as early as possible. In fact, I know interns who have been in the same company for three or four straight years. They get to know the company, the company knows them, and they usually get hired because they already understand the culture and the people in the organization.

> Don't view Internships as a "senior year thing." View them as an "every year thing."

If you are a senior or just graduated, maybe your college path looked like the one above. Or maybe your path looked nothing like that. Either way, now it's time to hone in on a career. So, how do you do that? Let's start with your major.

Your Major Does Matter

Over the years, I've heard a lot of advice that sounds like this: *"Just get out there and try things out. You'll discover what you like one day."* I agree with this advice, up to a point. Yes, it's important to figure out what you really want to do. But I will also tell you that the faster you find your niche and become skilled in that niche, the faster you will be promoted and get noticed by the right people. The way to start this out right is to carefully select your major. Your chosen major should be a great indicator of the type of work or industry in which you want to build your career and your reputation.

Does the thought of picking your career path in college fill you with fear? It does for many—but it's not as hard as some students make it. During the four (or so) years you spend in college, you have plenty of opportunities to research jobs and industries as you participate in class projects or group work. As long as you have to do the work to get the grades, you might as well focus your efforts on the industries, companies, and roles that interest you the most.

There is an almost endless wellspring of knowledge about any industry under the sun at your disposal in college. Many of your professors were in the work world (or still are), and would be happy to share their knowledge with you and honestly answer your questions about their industry. As an added bonus, when you seek out your professors' guidance outside of class, you will ensure that you get yourself noticed and remembered as more than just another warm body in a seat; and you never know how that may help you in the future.

You are already aware that colleges bring in guest speakers on a regular basis. The best way to know which ones you can't miss is to be a regular at the career center or stay up to speed on the goings on in your department. You can get a good glimpse into an industry or profession through these types of events. And many times, there will be a Q & A session at the end of these lectures so you can get answers to your questions about a specific role or function.

Talk to people who have been in their careers for varying lengths of time. The 20-year and 30-year veterans are great resources, but you also want to seek out those who have been in their profession for three to five years. They will be more likely to tell you how it really is when you are just starting out. twenty-year veterans have a different perspective on the day-to-day work, but they can definitely tell you what companies are looking for and what it takes to be successful.

It's your responsibility to think outside the box. Don't pick a major because your best friend, girlfriend, or father picked it. Talk to your parents or friends of your parents; or better yet, make a lasting impression in front of your professors by suggesting certain professionals they could invite in to speak to their class. That's a win-win situation. You'll learn more about a profession that interests you AND you'll look like a go-getter to your professors.

> Seek the opinions of both veterans and rookies to get the most well rounded view of an industry or profession.

Together, all of these things can be powerful weapons for choosing your major with confidence rather than with an attitude of, "Well I guess this is just about as good as anything else."

Now let's take a look at another scenario: Pretend you are a corporate recruiter. You recruit for Company X, who has told you to be on the lookout for a good marketing person. You are currently considering two candidates who are both relatively new to the corporate world, and both of them have worked for 3 different companies in 3 years. Take a look:

Candidate #1: Rico

Company A:
Worked for 8 months as a Customer Service Assistant

Company B:
Worked for 18 months in the Travel Department

Company C:
Worked for 12 months as a Sales Analyst

Candidate #2: Chelsea

Company A:
Worked for 12 months as a Social Media Analyst

Company B:
Worked for 18 months in an Advertising Agency

Company C:
Worked for 12 months as Marketing Analyst

Who looks better? Chelsea has been engrossed in the world of PR and marketing to some capacity for her entire career, whereas Rico has department jumped. Chelsea is obviously more appealing on paper, and if her interview skills are polished and sharp and she has the personality and the attitude company X is looking for, she will be the clear choice over Rico, unless the company specifically wants someone with different experiences (but my guess is that does not happen very often).

There will be some points in your career, especially when you're first starting out, when you may not have much say as to how long you hold a certain position. In fact, sometimes companies like to rotate their newbies around to give them a taste of different departments as a part of the orientation process. But that is usually done by a small group of companies with a select group that they are grooming.

The most important thing to remember is that the faster you figure out where you want to stay, the better it is for your resume—and each and every decision you make in the first few years after college will follow you throughout your entire career.

Coach's Corner

What Does Your Resume Say About You?

Have you ever had a job or internship? (Even cutting the grass in the summer or babysitting counts for this exercise.) Write down the following things about at least three positions you have held in your life up until now:

1. Title of position
2. Amount of time at position
3. Industry or area position was held
4. Positive outcome or result from your time in that position (made extra money, contributed winning idea, solved a problem for boss, etc.)

Position #1 Title:

Duration of Job:

Industry:

Positive Outcome:

Position #2 Title:

Duration of Job:

Industry:

Positive Outcome:

Position #3 Title:

Duration of Job:

Industry:

Positive Outcome:

Now, take a moment and look at your resume from the eyes of a corporate recruiter. Pretend you've never met the person whom this resume represents. Write down the first thoughts you would have about this person (who happens to be you) based SOLELY on the information above:

Do you like the impression you make on paper? If you don't, then luckily, you're young with plenty of time to change things so that you like how you look on paper—*because it DOES matter.*

Based on this better understanding, answer these five questions to help you determine which career is right for you:

1. What gifts and abilities do I have?

2. What do I do effortlessly that, at my worst, is better than others trying their best?

____

____

____

3. What do I truly desire to do?

____

____

____

4. If I knew I could not fail, what would I do?

____

____

____

5. What do I not like to do?

____

____

____

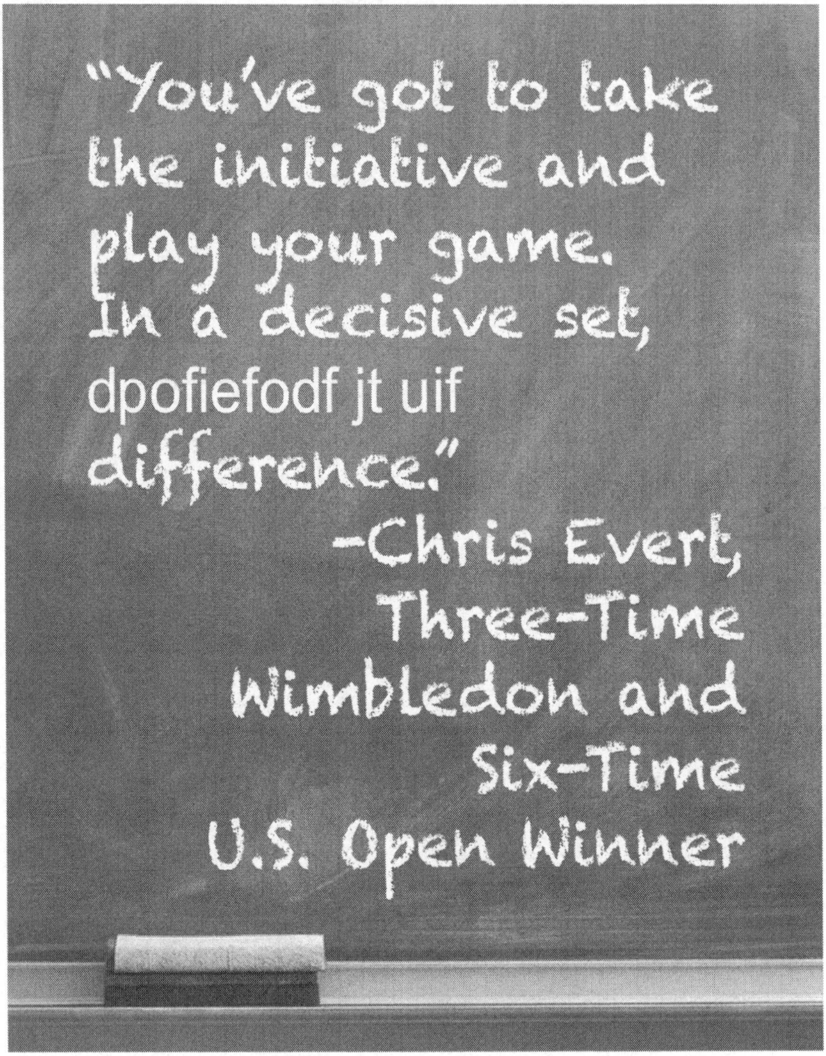
"You've got to take
the initiative and
play your game.
In a decisive set,
dpofiefodf jt uif
difference."
-Chris Evert,
Three-Time
Wimbledon and
Six-Time
U.S. Open Winner

Chapter 4

How to Play the Game: Determining Your Winning Approach

"The secret to success is only a secret to those who don't ask!"

-Stephen Krempl

As coaches and players get ready for an upcoming game or match, they have a decision to make. They decide whether they believe they will win or think they will lose because they are not good enough—and their decision will show in the way they practice and prepare. Of course, it doesn't always turn out exactly how they planned, but that doesn't change the fact that their approach matters. Can you imagine an NFL team going into the Super Bowl chanting:

"Alright! Let's barely survive this game!"

"Go team! Let's do just enough not to totally embarrass ourselves!"

That doesn't happen. They approach the game with confidence, and each and every time they practice, they know they want to win or they make sure they know how to cover their weaknesses. Why not approach your career in the same manner? No matter in what role or function you end up, you must decide at the beginning how you are going to approach it. Your success will be determined more by this than by any great knowledge that you have acquired. In fact, it will ultimately determine the path your career takes.

Not long ago, I was speaking to a long-time acquaintance, Jane. She had asked me for some career advice, and as I was speaking, she stopped our conversation mid-stream and asked, "Hey do you remember Susan Porter?"

"Of course I do," I replied. I met Susan around the same time I met Jane, and Susan was the kind of person you remembered.

"Well, she just made VP."

"Great!" I replied enthusiastically.

Jane was a senior manager, which was an admirable position, but her next comment said it all. Jane sighed and said, "Yeah, we started at the same time and at the same level, but Susan is a real go-getter."

And it was true. Susan *was* a go-getter. I don't believe Susan is any more intelligent than Jane is. But she decided early that she wanted to "make it." And so Susan's approach was on a completely different level than Jane's. Susan chose a **TOP TIER APPROACH** (or Top Of the Pyramid approach) to her career—and that's what set her apart. Everyone is unique, with different priorities, which means the level of effort you decide to put in is completely up to you. Let's discover what that means for you and how you can take a TOP OF THE PYRAMID approach to your future if you really want to be *GREAT*.

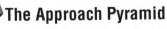

The Approach Pyramid

When it comes to the way you view and handle your work, your company, and your career (and really, everything else you do in life), there are four approaches you can take:

You can Survive. You can Cruise.
You can Contribute. You can Win.

If you're like most people, you have friends in all four categories, and you yourself may have used all four of the approaches at some point during your life and your time in college. Let's take a look at the approach pyramid:

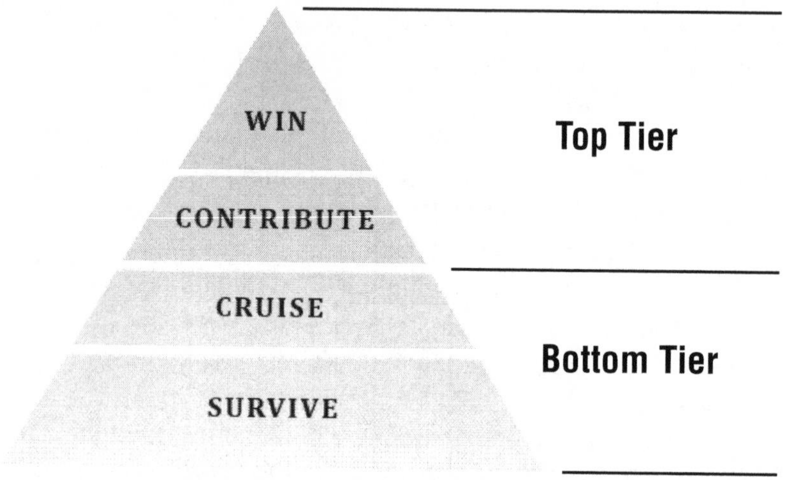

Behavioral Approach Pyramid

Some individuals have made an art out of justifying why they take a BOTTOM TIER approach to their work—why they are *survivors* or *cruisers*. Others try to take TOP TIER approaches—to *contribute* or *win*—but they may not know exactly what is stopping them. Ultimately, there is no right or wrong approach or intention; it really all depends on what you want from your career, current company, or role. Many people are content with where they are and what they are doing. But remember, this playbook is not for them; this book is for those who want to stand out. As you decide whether you are ready to take a TOP TIER approach to your new life outside college, ask yourself:

On what TIER are Tiger Woods and Peyton Manning?

Do Mark Zuckerberg, Bill Gates, and Howard Schultz take a TOP TIER approach?

If you've ever tried to get an A in class, did that require making more effort than the kids did who were content with a C? *Sure.* Of course, a lot of it has to do with your situation—some have to get good grades in order to maintain a GPA that is high enough to keep a scholarship, while others do it to satisfy their parents, and others are just plain smart. What is your reason for wanting to *win*? Are you prepared to make the decisions to get there?

If you have already landed your first job, or even if you are still a freshman with years to go before your career begins, one thing remains the same: *You have to decide how you are going to approach your position.* Are you going to take the job mainly because you don't want to starve? In other words, is your job "just a job?" If so, then you are on the ***survive*** tier of the approach pyramid. There is nothing wrong with that. Still other people accept a position and then set their brains to ***cruise*** control thinking, "Hey, I've got enough money to pay my rent each month. Yep, life is great." There's nothing wrong with that either.

But if you really want to shine in an organization, you must decide to be on one of the top two tiers of the pyramid, to either ***contribute*** or ***win***, which means that you are ready to help your company thrive and achieve more because YOU are a part of the team. And in order to do that, you have to do more and be better than your competition. How can you accomplish this? Is it through talent or hard work? We'll answer that question in the next section.

Talent Versus Work Ethic

Many would argue that the best athletes in the world are also those with the greatest amount of "raw talent." Others contend that you can become the best if you are willing to practice hard enough. It's difficult to say for sure which camp is absolutely correct (it's likely a bit of both), but one thing is for sure. Even those with the greatest amount of raw talent still have to practice. Raw talent is, by its very definition, *raw*—which means it's in need of honing, shaping, and perfecting. So in the search to determine how much effort you think you need to put into your new career, let's take "raw talent" out of the equation for the time being. Instead, we are going to focus on the fact that the most successful athletes and business people in the world all agree on one thing: *Winning requires practice—and lots of it.*

> Regardless of raw talent, winning requires practice—and lots of it.

How much work does it really take to have a TOP TIER approach? Let's look at the approach pyramid again in terms of your college classes: You can ***survive*** a class and get a D. You can ***cruise*** and be content with a C. If you regularly ***contribute***, chances are you'll end up with a B. But if you really want to ***win*** and get an A, it will require a lot more work than a C or D, or even a B.

How about in sports? The level you want to reach in a particular sport (high school level, college level, minor leagues, professional) determines how much you practice. Yes, there is your level of raw talent to consider, but ALL professional athletes practice and put in the work to become great. If fact, the ones who are the greatest are generally the ones who get to practice early, stay late, and go the extra mile to become better than the rest.

The Mindset of a Champion

What kind of approach do you currently take to work and to life? You may think you take one approach to life, while others would say something else. The real question is what do others say about your approach to your work? And what do you want your colleagues or supervisors to say about you and your approach? If I came to your company one month after you started and asked your boss about you, I wonder if he or she would say something like:

"Wow, Monica is great. She really hit the road running. She's contributing at meetings, greatly benefitting the group, and truly helping the team win."

Or perhaps the boss's response would be more like:

"So yeah. James seems super nice. He's been on time and is trying really hard to understand his role here."

There's nothing wrong with his boss's description of James, right? It's acceptable. He's not on the chopping block about to be fired. But why be *acceptable* when you can be *exceptional* like Monica?

Your bosses and coworkers are judging you and placing you somewhere on the approach pyramid, whether they say it or not. In your first 30 days at a new company, people are deciding what kind of person you are; and after this unofficial and unspoken evaluation of you is over, most people will keep that opinion of you for a long time in your career at that company—unless you do something significant to change it. Over the years, I've seen countless numbers of people join my teams and my organizations. And in each instance, I decided within a short window of time what kind of approach these newcomers took to their jobs. Many times I said to myself, *"He's a nice guy, but he's a cruiser."* On what criteria do I base such conclusions? Think about this: Are you aware when someone is not really invested in a task or activity? Well guess what? People also notice it when *you* aren't committed.

When a new employee packs up and shuts down his computer at 4:45 every day, I know he's not really there to win. Maybe right now you're thinking, "But Stephen, if my workday ends at 5:00, what's wrong with winding things down at 4:45?" You're right—there's nothing *wrong* with it at all. ***But it's not the behavior of a champion.*** The most elite athletes push until the last second. They don't check out 15 minutes before the end of the game; and if they did, they certainly wouldn't be on top for much longer.

Will You Contribute or Win?

Do you think that people who cruise or survive would ever get promoted over those who contribute and win? And do you think that BOTTOM TIER candidates stand a chance against their TOP TIER competition in the battle for the best positions? When I used to interview candidates for positions on my teams, I could usually tell during the interview stage what approach a candidate would take to his or her work. When asked, "Why do you want to join our organization?" I heard this response over and over again: *"Because I want to contribute."* That response is okay, but this is how I translated it: *"I just want a job. I think I'm pretty good, and I like your pay scale."*

Even if you don't yet know exactly how you will make a difference at a company, you can act like you do. You can approach every interaction with a winning attitude and word your responses to questions about why you joined the company with statements like, " We have a winning company..." or "We have stand-out products..." This sounds much better than the clichéd response, "Because I want to contribute."

The TOP TIER approach can be applied to your life, no matter where you are right now. For example, you can visit your professor during his office hours and say, "Professor Smith, I want to get an A in your class. Can you tell me exactly what I need to do to get an A?" You won't get the same response you want from every professor. But certain professors—those who appreciate ambition and effort—might say something like, "Okay, Johnny, if you do these five things, you will have a higher chance of earning an A." Then if you do everything he listed, it's going to be hard for Professor Smith not to give you an A (unless you bomb the exam).

> Champions push through to the last second. And they dont just contribute —they win.

It's no different in your new organization. You can walk into your supervisor's office at the end of the first week and say, "I really want to be successful in this company. Tell me what I need to do to be successful." Your supervisor could say, "The successful people in the company do this and that..." And then that is exactly what you do.

The secret to success is only a secret to those who don't ask! And it really all comes down to this—when you begin your new career:

- Are you going to survive by clocking in and clocking out and doing just enough not to get fired?
- Are you going to cruise with a mindset of, "I know I could do something more if I really tried, but I'm content to stay where I am."
- Are you going to contribute, which means you will have to be a little more involved, and at times, actively seek out ways to participate?

- Are you going to win by approaching your new career with an attitude of, "What can I do to make a difference and truly stand out from my competition?"

If you do choose to take a TOP TIER approach to your work, then this playbook is the jumpstart you need to get your career off and running on the right track.

Coach's Corner

Timeout! Let's Assess Your Approach

Think of four major events in your life so far. They could be anything that shaped your life or played a part in some outcome in your past and now your present. They could be things like: A major presentation in class, the big game in high school or college, your first job interview, your college entrance essay, or anything in between. List those events in the lines below:

Event #1:

____

____

Event #2:

____

____

Event #3:

____

____

Event #4:

____

____

Now, take a look at the approach pyramid again:

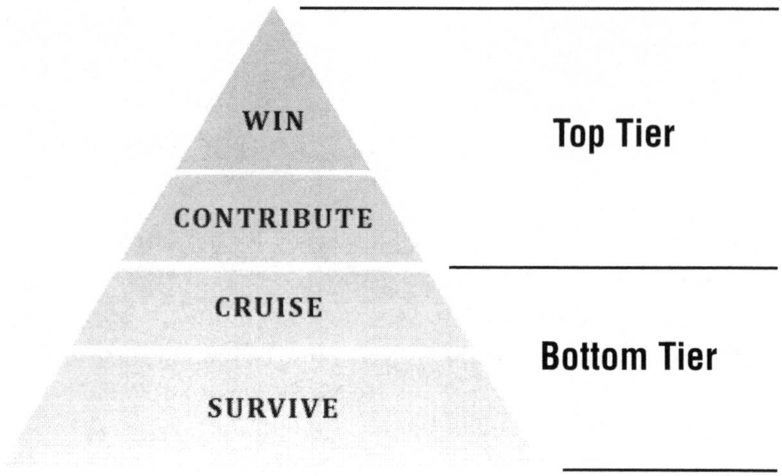

With the approach pyramid in mind, write down what approach you took for each of those major events. If you chose WIN or took the top tier approach for all of them, then wow, you're already on the right track. If you chose anything besides WIN for any of the 4 events, then on the lines below, briefly detail how taking a TOP TIER approach may have changed the outcome of one or more of the events. Most importantly, why did you choose that approach?

Event #1 Approach:

____

Why:

____

____

Event #2 Approach:

Why:

Event #3 Approach:

Why:

Event #4 Approach:

Why:

"Today I will do
what others won't,
so tomorrow I can
accomplish what
others can't."
- Jerry Rice, #1
NFL Wide Receiver
of All Time

Chapter 5

Having The Ideal Mindset: Getting Into Your 5% Zone

"95% of the time, you can be who you are at work. But 5% of the time, you need to step up... in order to stand out."

-Stephen Krempl

When it comes to staying in the zone, some athletes seem to have more pressure than others. For example, if Roger Federer loses his focus on the tennis court, everyone knows it, and it will probably cost him a game or even a match. But if a defensive lineman loses his focus and misses a block, it could go unnoticed, depending on the play. If a right fielder gets sick, there is another player ready to take his place for the next game. But if a professional snowboarder injures her leg, no one else can run the course for her—she's just out of luck. Like it or not, solo athletes are in the spotlight 100% of the time, whereas team players can rely on others during moments of lost focus or some unforeseen interference.

When you go to work for a company, you are joining a team. That means that everyone on the team is responsible for its success. That doesn't mean that you can sit back and cruise while everyone picks up your slack. What it *does* mean is that no one person has to be "on" all the time. However, there are situations that are more important than others. In fact, there are a select number of instances when it's absolutely critical to your success that you get in the zone. It's called the 5% Zone—and that's what this chapter is all about.

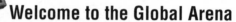

Welcome to the Global Arena

Do you have a plan for taking charge in the global arena? If you don't, then the person in line before you or after you will—and that individual will get the jobs and promotions that you want. Depending on where you live and attend school, things may or may not look all that *global* to you. But I guarantee that if you want to work for a successful company, your competition will come from around the world. For example, if you live in Seattle, Washington, you may want to work for Microsoft, Amazon, or Starbucks (who all have headquarters there). But you aren't competing against people from Seattle or even the United States. ***Your competition comes from every corner of the globe.***

This worldwide competition means that you have to be *the best* in order to get the jobs that everyone else wants. Now, the good news is nobody in the world is learning the stuff you are learning right now, which is to your obvious advantage. And because you are reading this book, you now have a head start over the competition.

When you are the best, you think differently than everyone else. Usain Bolt is the fastest 100-meter runner in the world right now. Do you think he steps up to the blocks thinking, "*Oh no, I hope I don't screw this up. What if I come in second place or take off too quickly before the gun goes off?*" No! He's thinking, "*I'm the fastest in the world. I'm going to blow these guys away and break another record.*" It's no different in the corporate world. In order to be the best, you have to think like the best. You have to think like a champion.

So how can you be the best and stand out from everyone else?

It's actually sounds kind of exhausting, the thought of having to be "on" all the time and watch out for the competition every step of the way. But remember, you are part of a team, and no team member gives 100% effort for 100% of the time. (No one could keep up that kind of pace!) That's why it's not as difficult as it sounds. In fact, it doesn't require you to change who you are or change the way you think or act—most of the time. You just have to change your actions and thoughts 5% of the time.

Not a 100 percent change.
Not even a fifty percent change.
Just a five percent change.

That's right, 95% of the time you can be who you are at work. But 5% of the time, you need to step up. I call this operating in your **5% Zone**. What does a 5% difference look like for you? Let's say you are not a morning person. You've tried getting to bed early, drinking strong coffee, and taking cold showers, but you just don't feel like yourself until after 9:00 a.m. This morning, however, you have a critical, all-team meeting. The VP of Marketing will be there, and so will all of your supervisors. The meeting starts at 8:00 a.m. *sharp*. This is a 5% moment. On most days, does it matter that you are a little sluggish for the first hour or so? Probably not. But for this special meeting, you better be there and be on point, ready to contribute, solve problems, and stand out.

The Four Zone Rules for Standing Out

Finding your 5% Zone is critical to your future and to your career path. If you know you want to succeed and you've chosen a TOP TIER approach, the next step is to identify activities that will fall within your 5% Zone and then choose one or more of these four ways to stand out during those moments. I call these the four Zone Rules:

1. Be Prepared
2. Add Value
3. Be Different
4. Be Proactive

In every important work situation (especially the 5% situations), you need to think about how you can add value, be original, and proactively solve problems. After all, these are the reasons you were hired in the first place.

Let's say you have to prepare for a meeting on ways to improve efficiency within your department. You determine beforehand that this is a 5% meeting, not just your weekly meeting. You decide to research what other companies are doing and call a few friends to ask what their companies have done in similar situations. In other words, you prepare so you can add value to the next meeting by providing that information to others. ***This is the essence of how you stand out from your peers.***

> Your competition is coming from every corner of the globe ...Are you ready?

You could attend the meeting without preparing, but then you will just be a part of the crowd. So if you determine that your intention is to *contribute* or—even better—to *win*, then the only way to do this is to be more prepared than the others. Such efforts will enable you to walk in armed with real options for standing out from your competition.

If you're going to work for yourself, standing out is arguably even more important because you're going to be out there on your own. People are doing business with *you*, not some faceless company, which means that you need be memorable so that when you leave the room, your customers say, "Wow, I really need to do business with her."

Now let's learn more about the four ways to stand out, whether you are working in a corporate environment or you are in business for yourself.

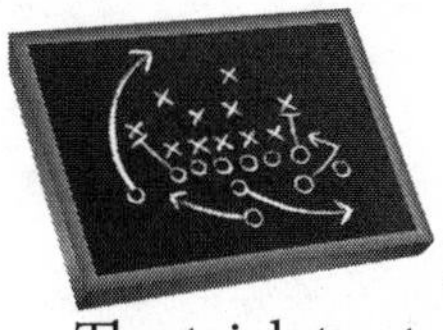

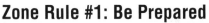

Zone Rule #1: Be Prepared

The trick to standing out is to do a little bit of everything, but not all the time. You want to be proactive and offer solutions when no one else is. You want to add value at some meetings (hopefully most) with well-timed comments. You want to be different with the strategic mention of a new technology you read about.

And at the foundation of all of this is *preparation*. Unless you prepare ahead of time, there is no way you can add value, be different, or be proactive. If you haven't prepared pertinent questions before the meeting, how are you going to confidently put your hand up and be the one to ask the right questions or provide the most helpful recommendation?

We're going to travel back in time to my days as VP of Global Learning for Starbucks. Let's say my friend Kevin calls me up at the time and says, "Hey Steven! What specific things have you guys been doing at Starbucks training on the issue of LMS (Learning Management Systems)?" I proceed to tell him what we're working on during casual conversation. Then at his next meeting, Kevin's boss asks the question, "What are the best companies out there doing about LMS's?" Kevin's hand shoots up and he says, "You know, I spoke to the head of training at Starbucks, and…"

Immediately it sounds like, "Hey this guy knows what he's talking about!" No one ever has to know that Kevin simply talked to his friend Steven for a few minutes (and if he needed more info, he could always get it later). He sounds like a pro. He sounds like he knows what he's talking about and where he wants to go.

Sure, you can always say, "I researched…" or "I read an article on…" but anyone can do that. It sounds a lot better when you can say you have actually spoken to somebody. Remember, you are only as good as the person who comes before and after you. So it's up to you to continually seek out ways to be different. And one great way to do that is to be better prepared than the next guy in day-to-day situations.

We aren't talking about "knowledge" here. If you are pursuing a career based on what you are studying (or studied) in college, I assume you know your stuff. You've taken your classes and you've learned the ABC's of your profession. But this isn't about knowledge. Anyone can read a textbook and get good grades on a test. That won't make you stand out.

What really matters is what you can do to promote your business and your team and help your boss. Let's say your boss needs someone to volunteer to lead a new task group. You've probably experienced something like this in college. When a professor asked for volunteers, how many hands shot up? Probably not many. So, if no one else's hands go up, what should your hands be doing? Going up!

Look for Ways to Connect

At a recent client meeting, I was going to be introduced to a leader in that organization with 600 people under him. As I was walking across the floor to meet him, I noticed everyone was wearing some form of blue colored uniform. But this guy was wearing a red polo shirt with three letters on it—T A&M. I knew this was Texas A&M, so I saw my chance. I came up to him and said, "Hey, how are the Aggies doing?"

He lit up. "Man! It's been an okay season. They are four-and-two!"

So I continued. "Do you think they're going to get to ten-and-two?"

"If we get to ten-and-two, I'll be over the top!" He went on for at least five minutes about his beloved alma mater.

At this point, I hadn't even introduced myself, and yet this guy and I were instantly good buddies—and we remained in contact since then, all because I noticed his shirt and got him talking about something that mattered to him.

Are the connections always going to be easy to spot? No. I'm not suggesting that you can connect in a personal way with all the influential people you meet, but when you keep your eyes and ears open and receptive, you will have the ability to find ways to connect in a quicker, faster way that sets you apart. My mantra is simple: Pay attention when you are in your 5% zone—more than you normally would.

Zone Rule #2: Add Value

Adding value is not hard, but it becomes a little harder when one thing stands in your way: **You**. Your opinion of yourself will play a critical role in your contributions to your future organization. Here is an important formula to remember: Your self-concept affects your mindset. Your mindset affects your behavior. *Your behavior affects your results.* Here is what that looks like graphically:

Self-Concept ➔ Mindset ➔ Behavior ➔ Results

Most people won't tell you this, but it's true: ***Your results will never exceed the level of your self-concept.*** This means that if you are in a meeting and you think, "Maybe I should say something," but then you decide, "Nah, who wants to listen to me? I'm new. Maybe next time," then your results will always reflect those thoughts. And if you don't say it, chances are someone else will. Why not get the recognition and acknowledgement that you deserve?

You can add value.

And you will add value.

But first you have to believe you can.

How many 5% opportunities (or even 1% opportunities, the most important moments of all) do you think you'll have during your career? Obviously, as a percentage, those moments are but a small fraction of your time in the work world. That's why you'd better be ready when they come up.

I know this better than anyone because I'm an introvert by

nature. If you've ever heard of the MBTI (Myers-Briggs Type Indicator), then you know that there are two types of people: Introverts and Extroverts. And as an introvert, I'm just not a "speak up" kind of person. I actually prefer to hide. Because of what I do for a living and the top positions I've held, this surprises most people, but it's true.

Practice Strategic Extroversion. But just because you are an introvert doesn't mean you can't be *strategically extroverted* at times. You can speak up and take charge just as well as the biggest extrovert in the room. Then after the important meeting is over, you can unwind in your own way. Extroverts are the people who end a meeting with, "Hey! Let's go for drinks!" Introverts think, "I want to go home by myself, quietly watch TV, and recharge." *Who cares that you have to decompress after stepping outside your personality comfort zone for a few minutes, as long as you made a strong, lasting contribution?*

I don't accept the excuse, "You don't understand, Steve. I'm an introvert. I don't like to speak up." I do understand because I am an introvert; that's why I also know that it's no excuse. It doesn't matter how loud or quiet you are. You can find your 5% Zone, those moments when you must step out of your comfort zone to make an impact.

Zone Rule #3: Be Different

When you want to stand out, you've got to be different. *Your future company already has enough cookie-cutter employees.* Why simply add to that number? You must actively seek out ways to be different, and you can accomplish this by doing something as simple as participating and asking questions. If your normal 95% self tells you to keep quiet, that is exactly the time to speak up. If your mind screams, "Don't ask that question!" then immediately put your hand up. I know it's counter-intuitive, and you may be thinking, *I'd never do that in my college classes!* But we're not talking about college; we're talking about your future. And if you want to stand out, you might have to beat up that little voice in your head. If that little voice says, "Don't make eye contact," then make eye contact, especially if it is a 5% situation!

You can be different simply by the way you phrase a comment. Let me give you an example: You are in class and the professor asks you to relate a concept you just discussed to a current event or story from the news. He calls on the first person, whose response sounds like this:

> *"Uh, it um seems like companies are getting lazy and not wanting to care about their online customers as much as they should and more customers are going back to traditional retail because of it."*

Sure, that could be true. But now it's your turn, and you say:

> *"I read in the* ***Wall Street Journal*** *this morning that some e-commerce companies are facing two key issues: 1. They have sloppy customer service on the delivery end and 2. They have awful return policies. The solution the article suggested (and I concur) is that everyone in the process should be held responsible for customer retention and measured against it."*

Same basic comment, two drastically different ways to say it. Obviously, your comment will have a much better reception. Not only do you sound more intelligent, but you quoted your source as well. Maybe the other guy also got the idea for his comment from the *Wall Street Journal*. Well, too bad for him. He missed his chance.

Start practicing the **SIP (source, idea, point of view)** style of answering now, while you are still in school. Why wait and start practicing after you get hired? It's not that hard to be different, especially when so few of your peers are doing what it takes to stand out.

Lunch is Not About the Food

Here's a simple way to be different. Once you are in the work world, lunch is never just "lunch" when you dine with people from work or from your industry. Let's say somebody flies in from corporate headquarters and your boss asks you to take her to lunch. This is a golden opportunity for you. It's not lunch anymore. It's your chance to articulate your point of view and display your confidence. And it's your opportunity to show how different you really are and be able to connect with them (see chapter six for more on this).

Zone Rule #4: Be Proactive

When I was working for Yum! Brands, we had a worldwide human resources meeting in Asia with about 100 members from around the world in attendance. I was at a director level at the time, fairly high up in the company but certainly not at the top.

We were there to learn about the upcoming launch of our new culture program. But as the meeting began, I noticed some red flags right away. The verbiage used was highly Americanized; in fact, there were a lot of words that could not even be translated into local languages. This was a big problem, especially since it was supposed to be a program that embraced all cultures. If they rolled it out in its current form, it would have probably not have connected as well or at the very least confused much of the intended audience.

I saw a problem that needed to be addressed, and I had two options. First, I could have complained (Bottom Tier approach) to my boss's boss from the Dallas headquarters and said, "Dave, you don't understand. That won't work here. It's different here in Asia; and those guys in Europe and Latin America won't get it either."

Or I could take the other route (Top Tier approach), the route that only the best take—I could solve the problem. For the next twenty minutes, I did not pay attention to the meeting. Instead, I focused on how to fix this major issue. I wrote down the eight key words in the program and tried to create an acronym that people could remember. Within twenty minutes, I cracked it. Then, instead of complaining to my boss's boss, I put up my hand and said, *"Hey, Dave. I think we have a problem, but I have a solution for it. I came up with an acronym that will resonate with and make it easy to relate to team members from all cultures. It relays the same message you want to get across, and it's easy for people to remember."*

Then I went up to a flip chart and wrote down: BE PART CC, which stood for BE PART OF COMPANY CULTURE. Each letter made up the first letter of the eight principles and could be easily translated into different languages. Then I added, "If we roll the message out this way, everybody will get it." It was like a light went on in the room.

Four months after that event, I was working at the corporate headquarters in Dallas, Texas. *How did I get there?* Among other things, I solved a problem and stood out. There were a hundred other people in the room listening and probably noticing the same issues, and yet no one spoke up but me. I know I wasn't the only one who saw a problem, but I was the only one who offered a solution. You don't have to solve *every* problem for *everyone*—but I recognized a moment when the most important people from my company would notice me, and I took that opportunity to solve a problem.

Don't let your own head get in the way of solving a problem. Perhaps there have been times in your life when you saw a solution, but then you thought to yourself, "I doubt I'm good enough to solve anything, so I don't think I should mention this." Don't let that happen. Instead, find your 5% Zone and then use those critical moments to your advantage.

> Being proactive means you don't stand by while others solve problems that you should be solving.

The difference between an amateur and a professional is one major thing: ***Attitude towards practice***. The pros know that practice and learning are both life long activities—which means that you can never stop if you want to be on top. The professionals who get on top and stay there embrace this fact.

This book is just the start of what you need to know to achieve huge successes throughout your career. Everything you read and study from this point on is fuel to propel your career and keep you (as Lance Armstrong would say) ahead of the peloton.

Coach's Corner

Key Questions for Game Day

Important Points to Remember:

1. You are being judged from day one.
2. There may be a short "honeymoon period" at work, but even then, people are categorizing you—and you don't get to start over after the semester is over like you do in college.
3. Play to contribute and win, give it your best shot from the start, and put in extra effort up front.

Here are some questions that will help you hone in on what you want to do and how you can become successful faster than the rest of your peers:

What type of job or career do I really want?

____

____

What do I know for sure I don't like to do?

____

____

What are the 5% opportunities that will help me stand out in the company?

____

____

What is it you hope to gain in the future? **Take a moment and think about your career goals and why you are spending time reading this book. Write down what career goal you now have as a result of reading this chapter:**

____

____

____

____

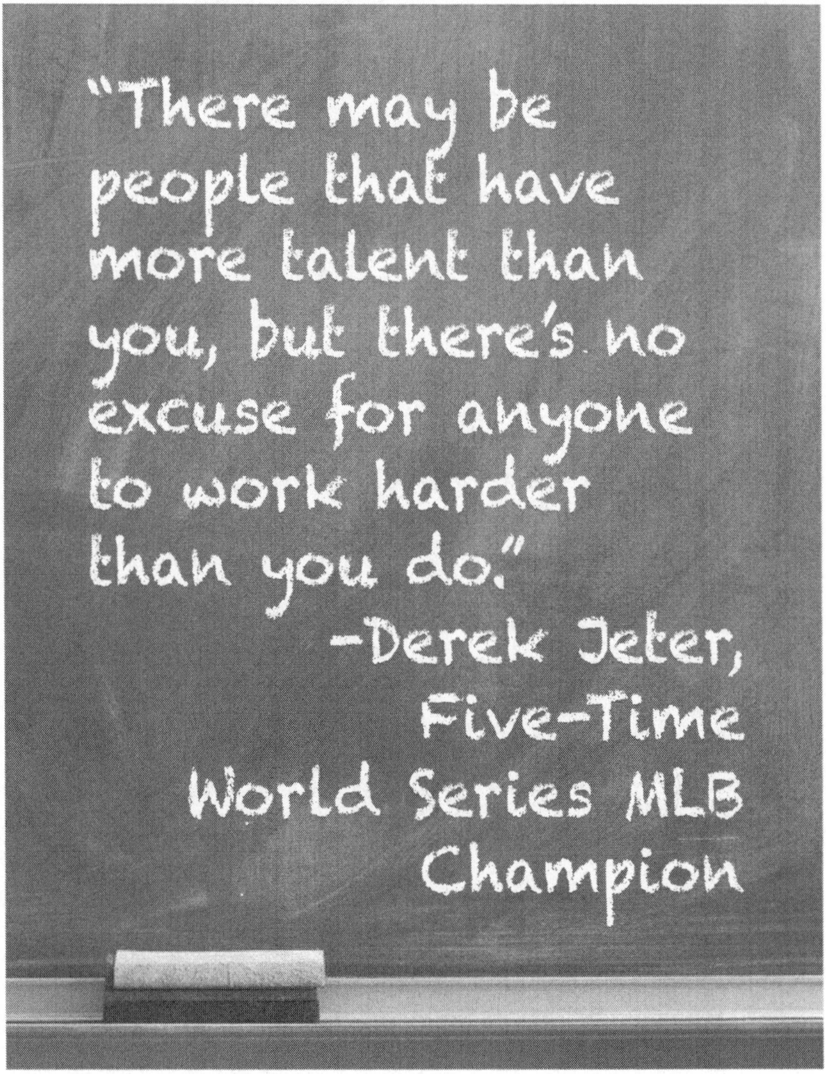
"There may be
people that have
more talent than
you, but there's no
excuse for anyone
to work harder
than you do."
-Derek Jeter,
Five-Time
World Series MLB
Champion

Chapter 6

The Skills of the Game: Competencies Employers Look for Beyond Your Major

"If you never step out of your Comfort Zone and into the 5% Zone, you will not get to where you want to be in your business or in life."
-Stephen Krempl

Coaches know it. Scouts know it. The best players know it. When it comes to selecting the starting lineup, there are a few skills and attributes that set the starters apart from the rest of the team:

- The starters are *confident*. They know they are the best at what they do, and their performance reflects that belief.
- They take *ownership*, which means that they know that they are the *only* ones responsible for their success or failure. When was the last time an athlete with a victim's mentality became known as a sports legend?
- The best players are *proactive*. They take charge when necessary, and they play to the strengths of their entire team.

The leaders at your future company are looking for the same things. In my research with *Fortune 500* executives, I've found that they all want their people to step up, take ownership, be proactive and share their points of view. However, many people talk themselves out of making standout moves. But whether you work for a small local company or a large multinational corporation, these skill sets are universally sought for, so it's time to figure out what skills of the game will land you on the starting team.

The reality of the workplace is this: After you get your first job, nobody looks at your diploma or really cares about what school you attended. I am not saying that higher education is not important; in fact, many times, the right school or degree is what gets your foot in the door in the first place. However, it is the way you express your thoughts, how you interact with various levels of the organization, your ability to gain people's trust, and how you get along with others that speaks more loudly than your alma mater ever could.

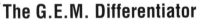

The G.E.M. Differentiator

You know that managers, executives, and CEOs are looking for special qualities in their employees, so how do you get there? It all comes down to learning the right skills of the game. There are seven skills that will set you apart from everyone else. I call them the **G.E.M.**, or **Global Executive Mindset**, behaviors. Take a look at the following diagram called the **G.E.M. Differentiator**. Each of the seven G.E.M. Skill Sets (found on the outside of the figure) are part of what helps make up the focal point of the diagram, which is your ability to STAND OUT:

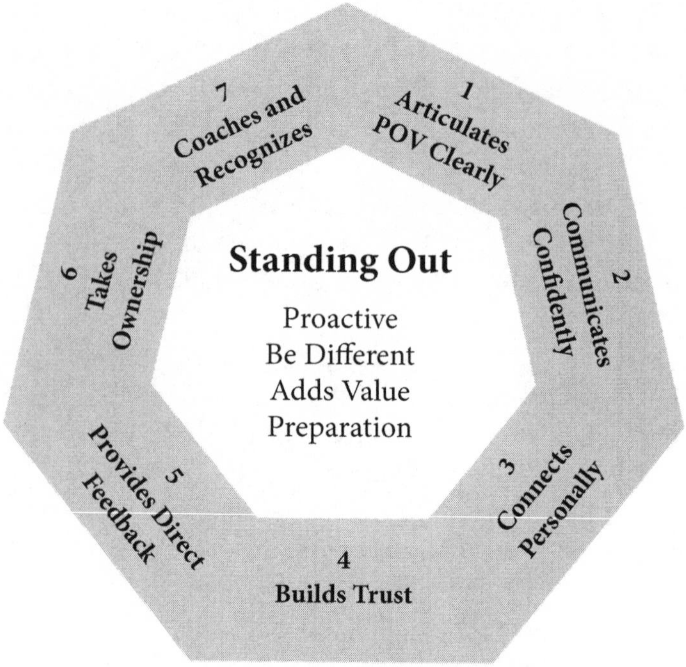

Do you know exactly how to communicate confidently, connect personally, and stand out in the corporate world? The G.E.M. behaviors will help you do just that. These are the skills that take your game from good to great. Here are the behaviors that G.E.M. fosters and promotes:

1. **Articulate Point of View Clearly.** This behavior requires you to get to the point, communicate clearly, and display cultural sensitivity.
2. **Communicate Confidently.** Confident communication includes asking timely questions, interjecting proactively, and sharing your valid points of view.
3. **Connect Personally.** When you connect personally, you know how to connect with people, leverage formal and informal meetings, and develop relationships within all levels of your organization.

4. **Build Trust.** This behavior includes the ability to meet commitments, act with integrity and influence at all levels within your organization.
5. **Provide Direct Feedback.** This can include pushing back with appropriate assertiveness, sharing any negative views early, and providing sensitive feedback.
6. **Take Ownership.** This includes showing initiative, suggesting new ideas, and willingly participating on teams.
7. **Coach and Recognize Others.** When you master this behavior, you can help others achieve their goals, guide and mentor others, and recognize and reward the efforts of others openly.

Does adopting a *Global Executive Mindset*, mean that you have to focus on all seven of these behaviors all the time? Absolutely not—you must simply choose to get in the zone just 5% of the times in your career when you need to increase your performance or intensity.

If you were a professional tennis player who was practicing for the U.S. Open, would you run around the court during practice wildly alternating from your forehand to your backhand to your overhead to your serve, or would you be better off practicing them one at a time? *It's the same in the corporate world.* No one can do it all at once—and besides, you don't need to. You simply have to take that extra step and practice one or two of your G.E.M. skills in 5% of the situations you face to generate explosive results.

Find those few moments in your career when a *little* extra effort will make a *big* difference.

It's not rocket science—it's small steps that lead to big changes. In fact, a 5% change in the way you act or think could lead to a 100% change in your life and career. So, let's dig into each of the seven skill sets to hone your game and learn how to stand out to the scouts [the corporate recruiters] and your future coach [your boss].

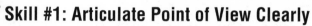

Skill #1: Articulate Point of View Clearly

When you are asked to share your point of view in a meeting, how do you do it? What is the best way to share your point of view (also known as your POV) that makes the most impact? And more importantly, how do you frame your statement up front to guide your answer and keep your audience engaged? To do this you need to use **SETUP STATEMENTS**.

We will discuss setup statements at other points in this book because I want you to understand just how important they are. Setup statements are statements that attract people's attention to your point and give you the framework to respond effectively! Here are some examples of good setup statements:

- "I have one important point to make (or two points or three points)..."
- "I would like to highlight..."
- "The key point you may have missed is..."

Absolutely *everyone* should use setup statements; they make all the difference when it comes to being heard and standing out from everyone else. How many times have you heard someone begin a statement with "Um" or "Uh?" It certainly doesn't make whatever comes next sound credible or even worth listening to. In fact, nothing says, "*I'm a mid-level hourly employee with no aspirations*" like, "Um, I personally believe..." Making setup statements is easy when you practice thinking and responding with them, especially if you pay attention to what the person before you is saying rather than rehearse what you are going to say in your head as he or she is speaking.

As you make your point, it's also important to get to the point! No one likes it when you hem-haw around the issue. Setup statements help you make your statement in a concise and direct manner while communicating in a way that everyone can understand.

Why is this a game winning skill? Your ability to articulate your POV clearly is one of the most obvious ways others can tell that you think clearly, have an opinion, add value to a discussion, and come across as the confident leader they need. Your polish and ability to act appropriately in different situations in multiple international settings will put you in a small percentage of great leaders. *Shoot for great!*

In addition to getting to your point and being able to communicate appropriately at all levels; you also need to be able to show cultural sensitivity, especially in dealings across the globe. Your style will not necessarily change, but the first few minutes of an interaction may have to change slightly. You have to **find out**, **adjust to,** and ultimately **respect** how things are done in a particular country.

For example, in many countries, acknowledging the most senior person in the room is appropriate. In fact, in some countries, his or her exact title and salutations need to be stated first (and correctly!) before you can continue. You have to know these things, which means that you either need to ask someone or pay special attention to what is going on around you.

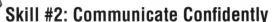

Skill #2: Communicate Confidently

When you speak up, remember you are consciously and unconsciously being compared against everyone in the room. So how do you distinguish yourself and stand out by communicating effectively and confidently? You need to be able to do three things:

1. Share your POV clearly.
2. You must also be able to share your point of concern (POC). It's important to help others understand why you may not agree with what's being said.
3. You must also use third party validation (TPV) effortlessly. This is a way of sharing your POC by using a validating statement like: "My customers are saying something different…"

You also need to be able to ask timely, impactful questions, know how to interject proactively, and be prepared to share your POV and POC and use TPV. To share your POV, thank the person who went immediately before you for making their point, and then add your point of view like this: *"Stephen, Zoe makes a great point. My point of view is..."* To share your POC, you can use a statement like: *"I have a different point of view"* or *"My idea is slightly different."*

Any time you have a differing opinion, it's okay to let others know. So, when you encounter someone with whom you have a difference of opinion, simply **Interject**, **Thank** the person, and then **Respond**. It doesn't mean you have to agree with everything, and there may be many times when you do not agree, but you can choose to respond with both professionalism and confidence.

Why is this a game winning skill? I have a different take on this than most people. Most would say that it is only common courtesy to share your concerns or your POV with professionalism. And yes, that is true; but the real key is that it is not only what happens IN the meeting or discussion that counts, but also what people are going to say or remember about you AFTER you leave. You want people to say something like, "Jill really added value here, and I liked her perspective" instead of "Steve was just being a jerk."

Remember, this is not what needs to happen at every single meeting. It would be nice if it did, but that's probably not realistic. These are your 5% meetings with key individuals in the organization or external parties who are on your 5% list with whom you need to have your best foot forward.

Displaying Cultural Sensitivity

Years ago, I was in Malaysia at a conference. On the first day after tea break, a training house was rolling out their latest material and introducing their founder's new book; and one of their trainers (from the USA) was on stage going through his introduction. Halfway though the session, their CEO walked into the room. He was a *Tan Sri*—which is a title given to only a handful of individuals in Malaysia—so he was important enough that everyone acknowledged him whenever he entered a room.

However, this trainer calmly proceeded with his presentation without acknowledging the CEO. The CEO walked to the middle of the large room, turned around, and walked straight out, as protocol was not followed. The host and others were scrambling to fix the situation and called an emergency tea break.

One could argue that the trainer did not know this protocol. However, if he had paid attention to cultural sensitivities (all countries have them) and took just a little time to find out what the nuances in Malaysia were, he would have known that all he had to do was stop and nod, acknowledge the CEO's name, and then carry on. Instead, he committed an international faux pas.

We simply spend too much time focusing on our own messages. So, pay attention and focus on what's going on around you, not only on what you want to say. This applies as much to a minor meeting as it does to a major presentation.

Skill #3: Connect Personally

One of the key skills that distinguish people with leadership potential from the rest of the crowd is your ability to interact and have conversations with people at different levels of your business. This includes the ability to show interest and give enough information about your own self to be interesting to others. Most students who attend my programs seem to have no problem dealing with peers who are on their same level or with those who are below them. They seem to run into problems, however, when they deal with professors, bosses, or supervisors in both formal and informal situations.

If this sounds like you, then your focus should be on developing relationships at all levels, which means you need to learn how to leverage both formal and informal meetings (i.e. lunches, time on the elevator, unplanned encounters).

All you need to do is to use questions following the acronym **F.O.R.M.**, which stands for *Family*, *Organization*, *Recreation*, and *Message*. It makes it easy when you have your F.O.R.M. questions ready to ask to determine what subjects they are most interested in so that you can get the other person talking and really connect.

Why is this a game winning skill? Knowing how to connect with people, leverage formal and informal meetings, and develop relationships at all levels is key to moving up in an organization. How many of you realize that the ability to develop relationships at all levels (not just at your peer level) is an important attribute? The question is how good are you compared to your local and foreign peers? Learn to overcome the mental issues that can surface when communicating with higher levels, which might sound like: "I feel a little uncomfortable" or "I don't know what to say" or "I don't know what to ask." And instead, prepare and be comfortable by knowing what to say and what questions you want to ask!

> Trust building is a continuous process; and yet it only takes a second to destroy a lifetime of effort.

Skill #4: Build Trust

Developing trust is one of the fundamental skills in any relationship you have in life. The truth about trust is that it takes time and multiple occasions when you deliver on your word to ultimately build trust. It is also an element that can be lost very quickly. As the saying goes, "It takes years to build trust and only seconds to destroy it." And in terms of business relationships, the process of gaining trust has three main elements:

1. *Delivering Results.* When you follow through with a promise or meet (and exceed) expectations, people learn to trust and rely on you.
2. *Building Relationships.* In order to have trust, you first have to form real relationships. This takes some time, so be patient and work on getting to know people at all levels of your organization.
3. *Showing Concern.* People can tell when you're putting on a façade or being phony, so practice building sincere relationships by showing genuine regard for other people's feelings and points of concern.

Why is this a game winning skill? Trust is the basis of all business interactions; and in fact, it is the basis of any human interaction. "Can I really trust this person to deliver on her promises or plans?" is always in the back of our minds. It is the same from a customer's point of view: "Can I trust this company enough to deliver what they promised?" You earn trust by focusing on all three of the above elements, which will then increase your ability to establish trust within and outside the organization.

Skill #5: Provide Direct Feedback

This is an often overlooked element of developing a Global

Executive Mindset because, well, not many of us really feel comfortable doing it. Providing feedback to peers and even to superiors requires you to push back with appropriate assertiveness. This can be challenging to do and requires the proper timing, tone, and word choices. But it must be done. Here are two ways to push back in a way that will be well received:

1. *Share negative news early.* If you have a POC or a problem, don't wait until too far along in the process when more effort (and emotion) is likely to be involved.
2. *Provide sensitive feedback.* As the old adage goes: It's not what you say, it's how you say it. This couldn't be truer when it comes to providing feedback. Choose your words carefully and be aware of how you come across.

When providing your POC during meetings or in one-on-one discussions, here are a few ways to start and examples of each:

a) Ask Permission

- "Is it ok if I share some feedback with you?"
- "Is it alright to share what our customers are saying?"
- "Is it ok to voice a slightly different view on this issue?"

b) Thank the Person and State Your POC

- "I like your idea. However, have you considered that this may have happened?"
- "That's great. I'd like to show you how we can increase results that will be guaranteed."
- "Wow, that is brilliant. Do we have time to consider another alternative that our competitors are using?"

c) State Problem and Suggest Alternatives

- "Jeff, this just happened. I can suggest two things we could do… What do you think?"

- "Kim, I am sorry I misjudged the impact of the... I have these options to get it right... What do you think?"
- "Jeremy, the item we were expecting did not arrive on time. I have a back up plan... What do you think?"

The impact of these alternatives depends on your tone, timing, and intention. People will know if you want to sincerely provide options or you simply want to shoot down their ideas. If you tell your leaders something went wrong, then don't just be a naysayer— instead, provide a solution.

Why is this a game winning skill? Most of the time, it's when you resolve a problem that you really get noticed, as things almost always never go according to plan. You just need to do the prep work required to provide solutions and not just throw the problem back at your boss. Leaders are looking for people who can solve problems—plain and simple.

Remember that in many cultures, getting feedback (even negative news) is expected and usually wanted early in the process. So figure out what the preference is in your company or with your supervisor. Most of the time it is an individual leader's preference, so determine which of your leaders sets the tone for feedback timing.

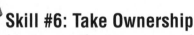

Skill #6: Take Ownership

Taking ownership in an effective manner that gets you noticed involves several major aspects:

1. *Show initiative.* This can include suggesting new ideas and picking up the slack where others on your team seem to be more hesitant.
2. *Readily lead projects.* You can't be afraid to step up and become the leader or project manager on an important task. In fact, when it's done right, there's

no better way to get noticed. But remember that when you are the leader, blame tends to fall on your shoulders. When this happens, don't make excuses—find solutions.

3. *Willingly participate on teams.* You can't lead every time. Sometimes the most appropriate way to contribute is to be a solid team member.

Why is this a game winning skill? Out of all seven behaviors, this one came out on top with the leaders I've interviewed over the years as the most desirable (and most lacking) attribute. Companies both large and small constantly have new projects, initiatives, rollouts, and community events; and someone has to be in charge of them. So when leadership looks around for someone to lead, do you readily put your hand up or hide behind someone else because you are just "too busy?" Yes, I'm sure you have your reasons for why you are not the right person. It's not the right time, you're too busy, or you're too new. Or maybe you've "done it before," and you think it's time to let someone else take the lead.

Leaders will eventually appoint someone, but I guarantee that they would prefer it if someone simply stepped up and took charge. And even if you don't get chosen, they will remember your initiative. So you have to figure out if that project or committee is on your 5% list. *If it is, your hand should go up fast.* Being proactive is one surefire way to stand head-and-shoulders above the others.

> No one ever seems to want to lead projects. So, how do you differentiate yourself? Volunteer to lead when no one else will!

Skill #7: Coach and Recognize Others

This is a facet that will definitely set you apart from your competition. If you can find ways to effectively help others achieve their goals, executives and colleagues at all levels of your organization will take notice. In order to successfully do this, you must be willing to:

1. Guide and mentor team members, which includes people *at*, *below*, and occasionally *above* your level.
2. Openly recognize and reward efforts. Don't be afraid to point out the contributions of others and praise them for it.

Everyone loves to be recognized for his or her efforts, ideas, or contributions. So the question is how much are you doing this for others? Have you ever thanked a professor or a supervisor for something he or she did for you? As author, leader, and management expert Ken Blanchard says: **"Catch someone doing something right."**

Many leaders will tell you that they got where they are today because someone took interest in their development or took them under their wing. Even though you may be new, you can still look for people who you can help develop or take under your wing to help them achieve their goals, especially in an area that you might be good at such as working with social media, dealing with technology, or connecting to younger staff members. And although you may not feel comfortable giving praise to others or receiving praise, but you must start picking this up as a good habit if you want to stand out.

> We all want recognition, so catch someone doing something right, and then say thanks!

Why is this a game winning skill? These three leaders sum it up best:

- "Recognition is the greatest motivator."—*Gerard C. Eakedale*
- "People may take a job for more money, but they often leave it for more recognition."—*Bob Nelson*

- "People often say that motivation doesn't last. Well, neither does bathing—that's why we recommend it daily."—*Zig Ziglar*

One final and important note: The most effective coaching and recognition come when it is planned. You can choose to do it spontaneously, but chances are you will be too busy. So plan when, where, and what you are going to do at your next opportunity.

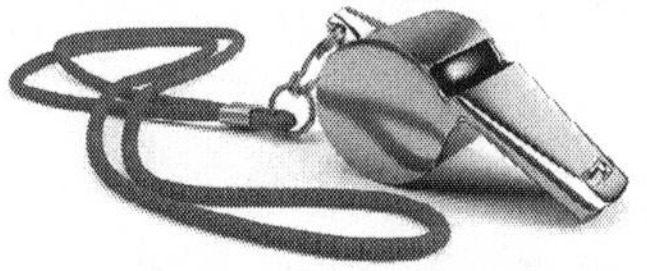

Coach's Corner

Take Your Game Skills from Good to Great

Like Jim Collins says in one of my favorite books, *Good to Great*, "Good is the enemy of great." This section is devoted to turning your skill level in each of the seven areas of G.E.M. from *acceptable* into *exceptional*. Now since you haven't logged many hours on the professional practice fields yet, I want you to think about the toughest class that you've had so far. It may be a class where the projects were highly competitive; and you had to really step up your game in order to stand out. If you are already in a job, that's great! With that in mind, answer the following questions for each of the seven G.E.M. skills:

Skill #1: Articulate My Point of View

How **GOOD** am I at getting my point of view across?

____

____

What more do I need to do to be **GREAT** at this skill?

____

____

Skill #2: Communicate Confidently

How **GOOD** am I at communicating confidently?

____

____

What more do I need to do to be **GREAT** at this skill?

____

____

Skill #3: Connect Personally

How **GOOD** am I at connecting personally?

____

____

What more do I need to do to be **GREAT** at this skill?

____

____

Skill #4: Build Trust

How **GOOD** am I at building trust?

____

____

What more do I need to do to be **GREAT** at this skill?

____

____

Skill #5: Provide Direct Feedback

How **GOOD** am I at providing direct feedback?

____

____

What more do I need to do to be **GREAT** at this skill?

Skill #6: Take Ownership

How **GOOD** am I at taking ownership?

What more do I need to do to be **GREAT** at this skill?

Skill #7: Coach and Recognize Others

How **GOOD** am I at coaching and recognizing others?

What more do I need to do to be **GREAT** at this skill?

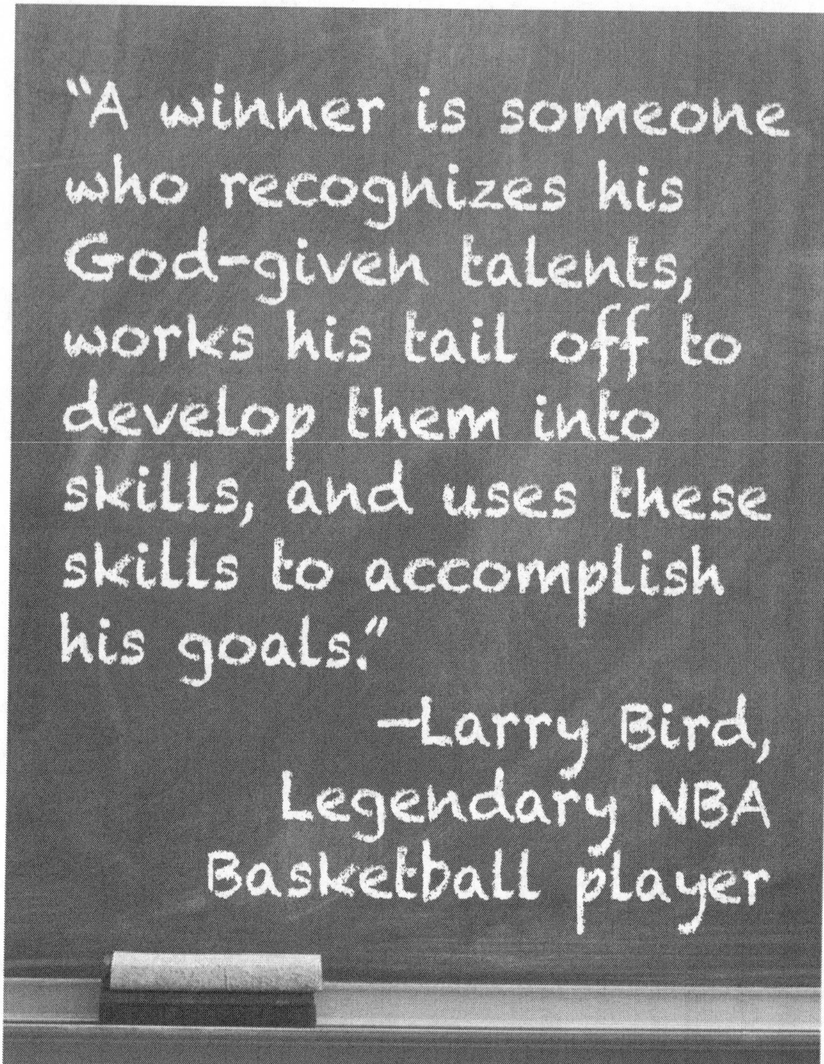
"A winner is someone who recognizes his God-given talents, works his tail off to develop them into skills, and uses these skills to accomplish his goals."
–Larry Bird,
Legendary NBA Basketball player

Chapter 7

The [Written] Rules of the Game: What To Expect When You First Join

"You have one shot to show your coaches what you're made of. Don't squander your first few weeks scrambling to figure out the rules. Instead, use that time to stand out."

-Stephen Krempl

Have you ever tried to play a game before you knew the rules? If you have, it probably didn't go very well—and you definitely didn't have much of a chance of winning (especially if your competition knew how to play better than you did). You've got to know the rules before you ever set foot on the court, before you put on the uniform, before you throw the first ball, or before your hand even touches the bat.

That's why it amazes me that so many college graduates enter the professional work world before they've learned the rules for winning in the real world. When you go in unprepared, you are voluntarily entering the "game" with a known handicap. You might as well add extra swings and misses to your scorecard right off the bat, because you are going to make more unforced errors than if you had just learned the rules before you started.

In this chapter we will cover the most practical things—the

basic rules of the game—that are largely defined by the culture of the company. And in order for you to be a contender and stand out, you need to learn these rules within the first 30 days of starting your new job. The rules you will learn fall into three categories:

1. **CULTURE**—Although all of the rules in this chapter could technically be lumped under the term "culture rules," the rules in this first category will include come of the most common traditions of the organization itself.

2. **TIME**—Every company also has certain rules about time built into their cultures. These include guidelines for how to handle everything from arrival time and prioritizing emails and voicemails to expectations at meetings.

3. **STORIES**—In this section, you will learn how storytelling is an integral step to building your credibility within the company and proving that you understand its culture, which you can start to do from the first day you arrive at your new job.

A few of the rules may seem obvious at first glance, but no company operates by the same exact set of guidelines. So, I am going to teach you some guiding principles, and then it's up to you to personalize each category depending on your current or future organization. Here is a quick look at each element within the three categories. As you learn the rules for this new game you are about to play, I will reveal exactly *why* you need to have these key elements of your new job figured out within the first few weeks:

Culture	Time	Stories
Energy Level	Meetings	Your Experience
Auidible Pattern	Start of Day	Others' Experiences
Space	Leave	Customers
Ownership	Weekends	Family/Friends
Stated Values	Responding to Email	Field/Frontline
Power Base	Responding to Voicemail	Management
Socialization	Responding to Text	Colleagues
Dress Code	Projects	Names

The most serious athletes know that they have one shot—one narrow window of opportunity—to show the scouts and future coaches what they're made of. If you spend the first few weeks on the job scrambling to learn all of the rules for playing because you never thought to learn them before you started, then you've used up your best moments to stand out and get noticed. The scoreboard clock is already counting down, so let's not waste any time and get right into the rules.

PART I. CULTURE

The word "culture" can mean many things. For the purposes of this book and your career, the **CULTURE** you are most concerned with is the one that directly affects how you go about your day at your new organization. There are some specific things you need to figure out when you start your new job, and the only way to figure them out quickly and effectively is to know what to look for before you get there. Here are the key elements of a company's culture and how to recognize them:

1. Energy Level

Every company has an energy level. Some are fast-paced and electric. Some are more low-key and laid back. And when it comes to adapting to the energy level of your organization, your own ideal energy level becomes secondary to the level within the company culture. Hopefully the supervisors at your company already selected you based on the fact that you match with their company expectations. This means that no matter what level of energy is your ideal *modus operandi*, you need to match yours to that of the company.

Don't like hearing that? *Doesn't matter.* That's how it works, so it's best that you know that now. Some companies are high-fiving types of companies. By contrast, more traditional banking or engineering companies are *not* the high-fiving types. They are more serious and buttoned down with a focus on processes and procedures; and when you walk in the door, you can actually sense that vibe.

So, let's say you are a high fiver or a fist bumper who talks really loudly when you get excited (all of which can be great qualities). If you work for a more process-oriented, serious company, you are going to have to *take it down a notch or two* at work. The opposite applies. If you are a stick-to-yourself kind of person who doesn't get excited about anything, and you start with a high-energy company, you must learn to embrace the occasional high five and enthusiastic meeting.

> No matter what level of energy is your ideal modus operandi, you need to match yours to that of the company.

Am I asking you to pretend to be someone you are not? Not really. What I'm really saying is that if you are not willing to do what is necessary to be one of the group, people will notice (and not in a good way). So, you have to match your energy level to the one within your organization. Pay attention and figure it out early on; and that way, if adjustments need to be made to your energy level to be more consistent with the company culture, you can do so right away. (So pay attention to your ninety-day plan, as this is one of the questions that you must find out during the interview.)

2. Audible Pattern

The second element of company culture is an extension of energy level, and that is the *audible pattern*. When you walk into the office or the building, does it sound like you stumbled into the middle of a Super Bowl party, or does it sound more like a golf tournament (where even the clapping is subdued)? Are people talking loudly, or are they speaking softly, maybe even whispering? Do you hear people shouting across the room to each other or are people's heads down as they work quietly?

There is no ONE right way to run an organization. Where *loud* works for some, *quiet* works better for others. It's not good or bad—but it's still something you need to pay attention to so you can adapt better to it. You don't want to be the one person on the phone with your brother or your friend saying (in a loud voice), "This place is SO cool! You gotta work here!!!" while everyone else is quietly working. Even though you may be oblivious to the volume difference, others certainly won't be. This is another way to stand out in the *wrong* way.

3. Space

What kind of workspace will you have at your new organization? There's almost no limit to what you will see. There are open environments full of cubicles or a sea of desks; there are companies where everyone gets his or her own large office; and there is everything in between. But no matter how big or small, private or open your new space may be, what's more important than size is what people actually *do* with their space. And one of the fastest ways to fit in is to personalize your own area.

In order to do this successfully, first take notice of what other people have done with their space. When employees have been at a company for a while, their office or desk becomes filled with personal artifacts, which can range from plants to photos to awards from the company. Then, based on how other people have set up their space, bring in items that will make you feel like you have been there for a long time.

Some small personal touches will make a big difference in how your coworkers perceive you. Look at it this way: Let's say you visit a friend who has lived in a house for a long time, but she still has boxes stacked in the living room, the mattress on the floor, and nothing on the walls. What does that say to you? There are only a few conclusions you can make from this: 1.) She is not planning to stay here long or 2.) She is lazy or too busy to prioritize. You don't want your workplace to give off either of those vibes. So one of the fastest ways to show people that you fit is to personalize your space (in the same way you probably moved into your dorm and started making it feel like home right away).

4. Ownership

Have you ever heard of the "ownership mentality?" For those of you who haven't, let me explain what that phrase means. When you are the owner of a car, you tend to take better care of it than if you are only renting a car for a few days. People also tend to treat their own homes much better than they do a hotel room or rental house. When you have ownership in something, you simply care more.

Depending on the size and nature of your organization, it might be privately or family owned, or it may be a public company. Whatever the structure of your company, the degree of ownership mentality present in the organization will greatly affect the company culture. Companies with a stronger sense of ownership can sometimes be thriftier in nature, while others are more lax about discretionary budgets. Some companies have a mentality of, "We act like owners, and so we do not spend a lot of money here." In these cases, employees tend to pay for things themselves that other companies often pay for such as meals, donuts for meetings, or birthday gifts.

Again, no SINGLE way of operating is better than another; it all depends on what works for your organization. Just watch how people talk about ownership and how they choose to spend work-related dollars—and then act accordingly. This is another good question to have prepared if you haven't joined an organization yet.

5. Stated Values

Plaques on the desks. Banners in the break rooms. Engraved walls in the reception area. When you walk into some companies, it's pretty obvious who they are and what they value most, because they put it up for all to see. A company may have its seven leadership qualities posted in all meeting rooms or its ten cultural values and mission statement hanging in the reception area. And if it was important enough for them to take the time and money to display it, then it's important for you to take notice—and then talk to people about what you see displayed.

> When you have ownership in something, you simply care more.

Perhaps the mission statement is the company's true driving force, or maybe you will discover that it's "really not all that important" or "no one pays attention to that anymore." Either way, it's better to ask and find out before you assume anything. You need to find out how things really work because sometimes the stated values and real values are different.

In Starbucks, they proudly display their *Green Apron Behaviors* everywhere, which are: Be Welcoming, Be Genuine, Be Considerate, Be Knowledgeable, and Be Involved. What does this tell you? It means that these behaviors play a significant role in their culture. If you see a credo or a set of principles that you are not familiar with, then find out what it means and how important it is to the company by asking your colleagues how they affect the culture and the way people operate.

If you were to walk into the Starbucks headquarters or even in the stores and ask anyone about the *Green Apron Behaviors*, that person can probably recite them and then tell you how they affect the culture. I recognized this fact right away, so one of the first things I did when I started working there was to give a *Green Apron Recognition Card* to someone on my team at the first meeting I attended. What did that do for me? Instantly, I could sense the "Hey, he's one of us" vibe. It's important not just to settle in, but also to do it quickly—and taking note of important culture cues (like plaques and mission statements) is a great way to accomplish this.

> You need to find out how things really work because sometimes the stated values and real values are different.

6. Power Base

Who holds the real power at your new organization? If you automatically assume it's the *big* boss, then you are probably in for some *big* surprises. When you arrive at your new job, it's important to determine who has the most power and sway on your floor or your department, and sometimes it won't be the person you think it will be. You can determine this by watching how people respond to others. Sometimes the people with the most power are members of the administrative staff (often called the gatekeepers). Of course, it could also be a manager, director, or even someone lower in the hierarchy.

Identifying the power base is an important but often overlooked step in your orientation process. For starters, it can be fascinating to watch the power struggles that ensue in most organizations; and secondly, it's the best way to ensure that you don't step on the wrong person's toes. It's also important to find out how things work, as decisions often revolve around the people who have the power base—and remember it does not necessarily have to be the highest ranking person, as the following story reminds us.

A Hidden Power Player

Barbara was an employee who had been at the organization for eighteen years. She had only reached the level of senior manager, but people quickly found out that she had the power base because she could pick up the phone and get right through to the CEO. They had started their careers together years ago; and although their career paths had diverged, they had remained friends, and he truly listened to her. For this reason, she had a lot of power and was a key influencer—and it had nothing to do with her position or title in the company. And you could either see her as a threat or a great ally who might be able to help you introduce your ideas.

7. Socialization

At some companies, your co-workers will become your new best friends. At others, people keep to themselves. The level of socialization—how people get along and interact—will vary widely depending on the company culture. Some teams go out together on Friday nights; others may be family oriented with planned activities like company picnics. Your new company may or may not have family days, holiday activities, or birthday parties. Other companies place a high importance on community projects as a group.

If your company does host social events, you must quickly assess how important these activities are to attend. Many people view such planned activities or company-related festivities as a chore. But if they are important to your boss or your CEO, then they better be important to you, too. In fact, you may even want to go the extra mile and volunteer to help organize some of them.

8. Dress Code

Would you wear a football helmet to perform ballet? What about a tennis skirt to go dirt bike racing? There are some obvious uniform rules that simply come with the territory depending on what game you choose to play. And in the vast majority of companies, the topic of proper attire will be conveyed (sometimes at great length) during the orientation process. But in some cases, a company's dress code may have a few less obvious rules as well. It's equally important to know and understand both the spoken and unspoken policies for your organization.

A major food group hired a senior human resources executive name John to join their Dallas, Texas office. Bringing him on board marked the first time that they went outside to hire a senior level VP, so he had a lot to prove.

As it turns out, John experienced one distinct disadvantage to being hired into a high profile position from outside the company. He may have missed out on an unspoken dress code rule. In the warmer months, we had dress-down Fridays. Taking from his experience at his previous company, John assumed he should wear jeans and a polo shirt.

Well, he got the polo shirt right. On his first casual Friday, he stepped into the parking garage elevator, and on the next level, the president joined in. Then when the doors open again, the new guy stepped in. The president and I were wearing our pressed khakis and polo shirts—and there stood John in his jeans. The president glanced at John and said, "Oh. Are you doing some gardening today?"

Poor guy—can you imagine the expression on John's face? Everyone who had been at the company for a while knew that the president thought jeans were *way* too casual, even for casual Friday. Spoken or unspoken, it was a big deal to the president, plain and simple. As you may have guessed, John never wore jeans again, but we never let him forget the day he did.

Maybe you're thinking, *"Oh come on. That's a bit much. It was just jeans."* But again, this is one of those cases when your own personal preferences don't really matter. What you consider casual may not be what the CEO considers casual. When in doubt, refer to the company rules, and in the long run, you'll be happy you did.

PART II. TIME

Time is relative. What's considered "right on time" for some may be "fashionably late" to others. And what's considered "a little tardy" to other people may be "downright insulting" to your supervisor. If there's one topic that you need to understand about your company QUICKLY, it's the timetable on which the company runs. Almost nothing makes you look worse (and nothing accomplishes it faster) than misunderstanding or abusing the most valuable commodity your company has, which is time. There are a few key areas where this is most important:

1. Starting Your Day

When did you schedule your first class of the day in college? I know some students try not to have a class before noon. (Who needs the morning anyway?) But in the real world, you can't schedule your own start time. So, whether it's a more relaxed 9:00 a.m. or more likely an 8:00 a.m. or even 7:30 a.m. start time, find out within the first few days what is expected of you in terms of promptness. Are people in their seats right on schedule? Is there a fifteen minute, unspoken "grace period?"

Just know that whatever time you decide to show up, people are watching. And if you habitually come in ten minutes after everyone else is there, this will affect how people perceive you, your work ethic, and your ambitions within the company. Some managers care more about this than others. During your first few days on the job, notice your boss's subtle body language cues when people come in late or are tardy to a meeting to determine whether or not this will be a sticking point with your new boss.

2. The "End" of the Day

Is it quittin' time yet? This thought plagues the minds of many from the second their lunch break is over until the official end of their workday. What do you think it says about someone when he or she is all packed up with one foot out the door at 4:45? Does that person have what it takes to be the CEO one day? Now granted, not everyone is CEO material, but if you are reading this book, you probably have some high expectations for your career.

That is why, when you are new to a company, I suggest that you stay a little bit AFTER other people start to leave. Will spending an extra fifteen minutes at work really hurt your day? No—and it will definitely *not* hurt your career. Try it for a few weeks and just watch what happens. You'll be amazed what a difference a few minutes makes.

> Whatever time you decide to show up to or leave work, people are watching.

3. Meeting Times

As a part of their culture, most companies have certain rules about the rigidity of meeting schedules. At some companies, meetings will *always* start right on time (maybe even a few minutes early), while at others, everyone meanders in within the first five or ten minutes and no one thinks twice about it. When I do training at a company, I've become adept at figuring out this aspect of their culture before the first meeting ever starts by noticing things like: Do people come in and sit right down? Are they milling around chatting with no real regard to the clock?

This is another aspect of company culture that is unique to each company. The point is to figure it out quickly; and perhaps more importantly, do so inconspicuously. If you are one who strolls in late when everyone else was five minutes early, then you are going to stick out like a sore thumb. It may seem like a little thing—and in some companies it may be. But if you find yourself working for a supervisor who likes his meetings to start on time, then it's not a little thing. Once you find out what's expected of you, you can do it every time without thinking about it and further solidify yourself as a real member of the team.

4. Weekend = Work?

Ah… Weekends. They're all yours, right? Not necessarily. In some companies the culture carries an expectation that some weekend work will be required. If you're thinking YUCK, then warm up to the idea now, because it may be a reality in your future. In one headquarters I visited in Bentonville, Arkansas, management meetings are always on Saturday mornings. And if you ask anybody who works there, they will tell you that they don't think twice about it, even though those meetings usually last the entire morning. That is the just the way their culture is and has been for years.

I am not saying that working on weekends is right, wrong or ridiculous; all I am saying is you better pay attention to this thing called *time* and what your company expects you to do during the week and maybe even on the weekends.

5. Response Times (Email, Voicemail, Texting)

If you are in a meeting and a text pops up from your boyfriend or girlfriend, chances are you should just wait until the end to respond (I'm sure they'll understand). But the same thing cannot be universally said about work-related responses. Many times, there are expected response times for emails, voicemails, and texts that are built into the company culture. How fast should you get back to people? You have to figure this out, because you can inadvertently offend someone or even appear lazy if you get it wrong. Some people don't care—but some do.

It's finally Friday afternoon, which means you can shut things and call it a day until Monday morning. *Not so fast!* Sometimes co-workers or your boss will send you emails on the weekend and expect a response—and they'll want it sooner rather than later. For this reason, you need to become aware of the expectations for how fast your responses need to be.

Let's say it's Friday afternoon, and your colleague sends you a message that ends with, "Get back to me on this as soon as possible." How soon should that be? And how does he or she expect the response? Is an email enough, or should you include a follow-up text or phone call? More importantly, is it okay to wait until after the weekend, or does this person need you to get it done now, before you leave? I know you probably can't even begin to answer these questions now, especially since many times, the answers will be case specific.

These are simply details to keep in mind—because no matter how trivial they seem, they do matter. You must establish with your boss and co-workers what they expect from you in terms of turnaround time so that you never leave anyone waiting for important information; and more importantly, you can become a valuable asset to your team.

6. Project Times

Whatever career you pursue, you will have work projects, both big and small. Because these projects are integral to establishing the value you bring to the organization, it's important to know how to handle them from a timing perspective. So, the first thing you need to do when you are assigned a project is to clearly establish the expectations for completion. You must determine whether the norm in your company is to have everything in on time, or whether there is an unstated expectation that things have to come in the day before or a week later.

> When it comes to projects, the only way to stand out is by delivering *what* is expected of you *when* it is expected.

In many ways, this process is not much different than it was in school, when you were assigned a class project and the professor gave you a due date. But the difference between school and the real world is that often times in the work world, there may be some "wiggle room" in the due date, depending on factors such as the importance of the project, the disposition of your superior, and the complex nature of the work.

Other times, you'll work your fingers to the bone on something, turn it in on time, and it ends up unseen, stacked in a pile with a million other projects. It may seem like all of your work was for nothing, which can make it tempting to ignore hard deadlines in the future. But when this happens to you (and it will, because it happens to everybody), just shrug it off as a "rite of passage" and get back to delivering *what* is expected of you *when* it is expected.

PART III. STORIES

The first two areas we have discussed are certainly important, but this one is perhaps even more critical to fitting into the company culture. Storytelling is vital because when you tell stories, people literally *hear* you fitting in. Now, some people may think, *what's so important about stories? Aren't they for campfires or sitting on grandpa's knee?* But in business, stories are far more than entertainment. The stories that you tell—from your own previous experience, from experiences in your current company, or even retold stories you heard from other co-workers, customers, family or friends—serve a critical role in your success at the company.

Why are stories so important to your career? They solidify you as a part of the team and prove to others that you know the inner workings of the company as well or better than anyone else does. The reason people know you have been around and know your stuff is because you have the "war stories" to prove it. And the faster you get the stories, the faster people believe you fit in and understand the company.

1. Build Instant Credibility Through Stories

Stories provide you with credibility when you need it most. Let's say you work for a bank at their headquarters, and as part of your job, you often meet with branch managers (the people who are on the frontlines every day). People on the frontlines often feel that the employees at their headquarters are tucked away and sheltered from the real action. So, how can you build standing with them in a sincere way that will open their ears and minds to what you have to say? Through stories!

Through a retelling of tales you've personally seen, experienced or collected from the branches, you can relate to the branch managers that you actually have an idea of what they experience on a daily basis. You don't have to pretend to know everything they know (this comes across as arrogant), but you have to be relatable and approachable. Stories are what allow you to reach across any level of corporate hierarchy and relate to almost anyone.

I was with Motorola for just over a year when I was invited to be on the presentation team for a program we ran for the general public. The other three members of the panel had been with Motorola for over twenty years. How could my twelve months of experience even begin to add value to their combined sixty-plus years of experience? *The answer, of course, is stories.* I had lots of them—some of them from my own experience, but many of them retold from the experience of others. After the training, many people assumed I had been with the company for a long time. It was amazing—and a real testament to the power of stories.

2. Build Up Your Story Arsenal

The sources of credibility-building stories are endless, so you must always be on the lookout for great ones to add to your arsenal. As a part of the orientation process, Starbucks sends all new headquarter employees out to work as a barista. Of course, I was no exception, so they sent me to work at a store in Lexington, Kentucky. It is important that all employees know how to make coffee, how to delight the customer, and how to see the business from the frontlines.

I decided to make the most of my weeks as a barista by collecting stories to use when I got back to headquarters. I knew that people would inevitably ask about my experience, so I wanted to plan out exactly what I would say that would be memorable and enhance my standing within the company. Reciting the steps for making the perfect latte or my favorite coffee wasn't going to cut it. I needed *people* stories and *culture* stories—and over the course of those few weeks, I found the perfect ones. The best thing is that now years later, I still use a few of those stories when I speak at colleges and companies. Here are two of my favorites:

Story #1: Celebrating a Father's Life. I was visiting a Starbucks in Louisville, Kentucky when a brother and sister walked in and asked to speak with the store manager (who happened to be standing right next to me). Of course, you never know what you're going to hear when someone says, "I need to speak to the manager," so we were braced for anything. The sister was already visibly emotional as she began, "Our father, John, came here every Wednesday for the past 2 years. Well, he passed away last week, and we found a whole collection of Starbucks cups as we were going through his things. Each cup had a little scribble on it with a smiley face and messages like, "Have a great day, John" and "You are great" and "Nice seeing you again, John" or a smiley face."

The brother then added, "Apparently our dad washed the cups and kept them because of the personal message on each one."

Finally the sister said, "We just wanted to tell you that you guys are amazing, and whoever served him must have made him feel special for him to keep those cups."

It was obvious that the kindness of the Starbucks barista or baristas had touched their hearts as they were grieving the loss of their beloved father. Making someone's day is an important part of the Starbucks philosophy, and this story really embodies the kind of impact they hope to have on people. The instant I heard this, I knew I would go back and tell this amazing story; and when I did, my coworkers recognized that I understood the culture and was going to fit right in.

And to think, I had been there for a whole two weeks.

Story #2: $100 Dollar Jim. The second story isn't even "my" story—I didn't personally witness it or experience it—but that doesn't mean I can't tell it. *If it is inspiring, conveys the right message, and builds your credibility, then why not share it with others?* After I started my two-week orientation at the Lexington Starbucks, my regional director Rich called and asked me how I was getting along. I shared the story about the brother and sister with him, which reminded Rich of something that he witnessed during his early tenure. He then told me a story about a customer he called $100 Dollar Jim.

> Stories are what allow you to reach across any level of corporate hierarchy and relate to almost anyone.

Rich was visiting a store in Chicago when the manager pointed out a man walking in. There was nothing particularly unusual about the man, except for one thing. Everyone who worked there seemed to know who he was. It was a lot like when Norm used to walk into the bar on *Cheers*. Each barista called out some greeting to this man whose name was apparently Jim. He then inquired about each one of them, about their last vacation or some other detail about their lives. Jim paid for his usual order, and then the most interesting thing happened. After he paid for his coffee, he casually dropped a hundred dollar bill in the tip jar. That's not something you see every day.

Later that afternoon Rich was visiting another store in the area, and he saw Jim walk into that store. The manager ran up to Rich and said, "Here comes Jim. He's our favorite customer." It was the same scene as from the previous Starbucks. Jim came in and called everyone by name, ordered a drink, and guess what? He dropped yet another hundred-dollar bill in the tip jar.

Jim obviously had a few dollars to spare, but most people who have a lot of money don't exactly go handing out hundred-dollar tips (much less two of them) at Starbucks. Rich couldn't contain his curiosity, so he went up to Jim and introduced himself, "My name is Richard, and I am the regional director. I noticed that earlier today you gave a hundred dollar tip, and then you did it again here. Can you tell me why?"

Jim smiled and said, "You know, I can't pay people to make me feel this good and make me such a part of their family."

It's the kind of story any company would wish for, as it displays the level of loyalty that they can only hope their customers feel. Remember, this wasn't even from my own personal experience, but I went back to headquarters and told the story of "$100 Dollar Jim" during my first meet-and-greet because no one had heard it before. They loved it—and of course, it further solidified the fact that I understood what the Starbucks culture was all about. I continue to use this story today!

3. Become a Master Story Seeker

You would probably guess that over the years, I've amassed quite a number of stories—and you'd be right. In fact, I'm still collecting them today and adding them to my arsenal; stories for any occasion, stories that will resonate with my audiences and build my credibility. And that is exactly what you need to do as well. It doesn't matter whether they're from your family, whether you heard it somewhere, or if you retell a story that someone else shared with you. In fact, one of the best ways to collect stories is simply to ask for them. People love to talk, so give them something useful to talk about. Here is my favorite question to accomplish this:

"What is your favorite story (experience) about the company?"

Your co-workers may pause for a minute to think, mostly because this question doesn't get asked as often as it should, so it catches most people off guard. But soon their eyes light up, and they begin with, "Well, back in the day..." And just like that, you have another story. This is a great way to build up your arsenal, especially when you are new and haven't had the chance to experience your own stories yet.

So, when the next meeting comes and somebody says, "Hey there, new guy. Why don't you introduce yourself?" You can say,

"I'm Steven, and I work in the benefits department; but what I'd really like to say is…" And then you dazzle with a short, fitting story. No one is expecting it and no one will quite know what to think other than, "Man, I better watch out. This guy's going to be my boss one day."

The three categories of rules we covered—culture, time, and stories—encompass the key information you need to know or find out in the first 30 days at your new company. Sometimes, simply opening your eyes and being observant is all you need to do to figure out the rules. But for the answers that aren't in plain sight, where do you find this information?

The solution is your colleagues. When you look around, most of the people you will see have been there longer than you have. If you don't know how something works or what the protocol is, you can ask the person leading your orientation. Ask the woman in the cubicle next to you. Ask the gentleman who strikes up a conversation with you while you wait for the elevator. Inside the workforce of your organization is a storehouse of knowledge just waiting to be tapped.

I'm not asking you to befriend every last administrative assistant in the building or bombard your boss with questions during his lunch, but you need to have a plan and keep plugging away at the information. Coincidentally, administrative or executive assistants are great sources for getting the scoop; but in general, just remember there are people around you who know the answers you need. Don't reinvent the wheel and try to figure it all out on your own. Ask for help. This has the added bonus of making you appear eager, ready to learn, teachable—and even better, promotable.

No matter where you are today—whether you are a freshman, you've landed your first job, or you're somewhere in between—it's never too early to begin your career in storytelling. Start looking for stories at your new company from day one. You have to deliberately look for them or they will slip by without you noticing.

What is the next place or event where you can plan to look out for a story?

Coach's Corner

The Art of Storytelling

What stories do you know or what experiences have you personally had that you could use to convey this message to the students on your tour?

Pretend you are giving a tour of your college campus. It's your job to convey to the prospective students that your university is full of rich culture and that the entire student body feels a loyalty to their school and what it stands for. You show them the buildings, the lunch facilities, the football stadium, and the dorms—but those are just buildings and structures. How can you communicate what truly makes your school unique and different, and how do you show them that it's the place they should spend the next four years of their lives? Stories are the answer.

What stories do you know or what experiences have you personally had that you could use to convey this message to the students on your tour?

What stories have you heard from other students, from professors, or from your parents that would help give prospective students the feeling that you really understand the rich culture?

____

____

____

____

____

____

____

____

No matter where you are today—whether you are a freshman, you've landed your first job, or you're somewhere in between—it's never too early to begin your career in storytelling. Start looking for stories at your new company from day one. You have to deliberately look for them or they will slip by without you noticing.

What is the next place or event where I can plan to look out for a story?

____

____

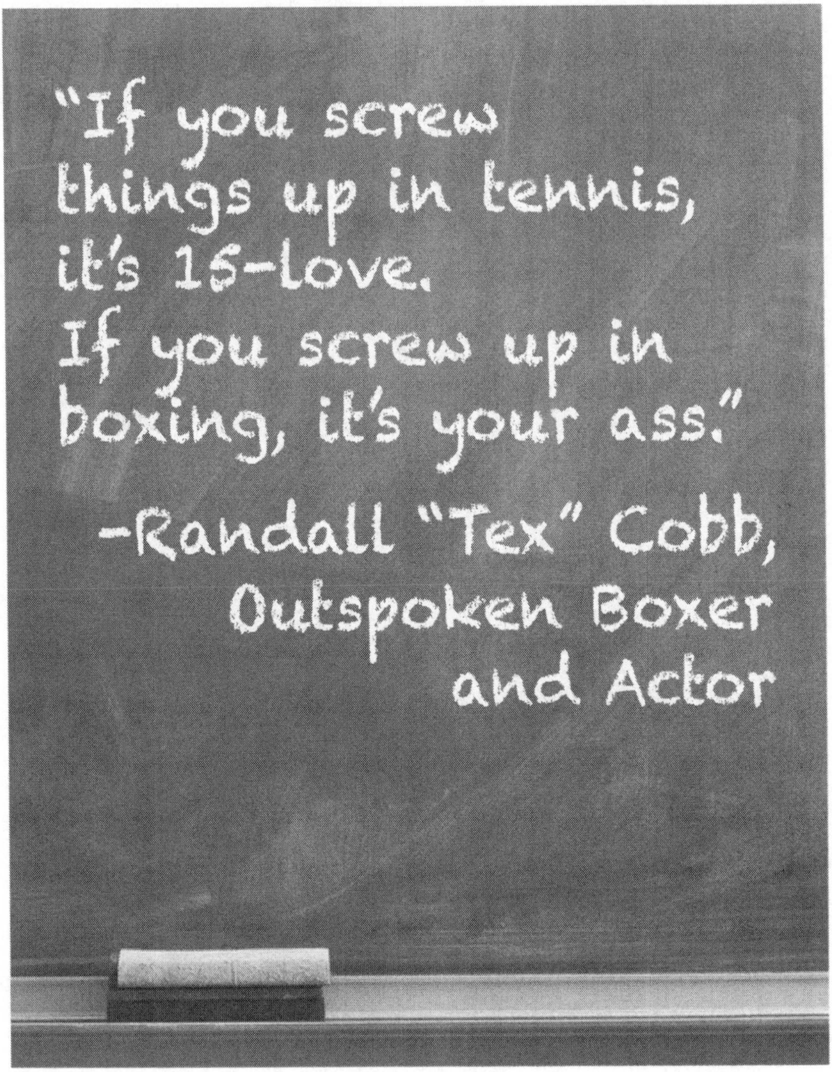
"If you screw
things up in tennis,
it's 15-love.
If you screw up in
boxing, it's your ass."
-Randall "Tex" Cobb,
Outspoken Boxer
and Actor

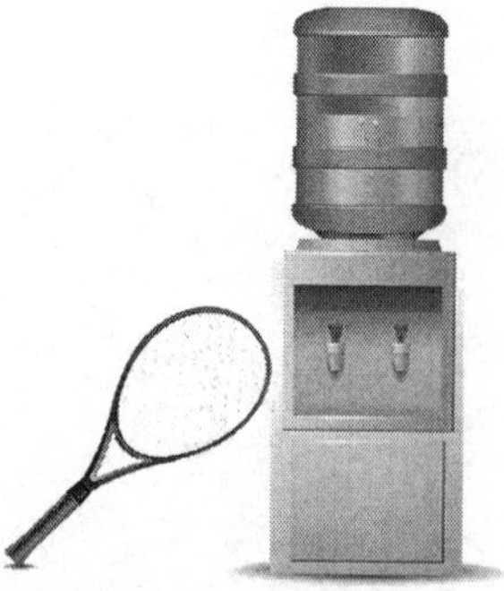

Chapter 8

The [Unwritten] Rules of the Game: What You Must Do to Get Noticed in the First Thirty Days

"Whether you are quiet, painfully shy, or both, it doesn't matter. You can stand out as much as anyone else. It's a choice."

-Stephen Krempl

What's the difference between a starter and a benchwarmer? Athletes have been asking themselves this question for years. The answer is probably complex and involves many elements, but one of them definitely has to do with the first impressions an athlete makes with his team and the coaches. So, what kind of impression makes a lasting impact in sports? Well, have you ever watched a WWE wrestling match? Some may call it a sport, while others may disagree and call it purely entertainment. Professional wrestling can definitely be rather polarizing—you either love it or hate it (or think it's ridiculous).

Whatever your opinion, no one can deny that those wrestlers make some pretty grand entrances. In fact, the more dramatic, the better. One of the most well known wrestlers of our time, Dwayne "The Rock" Johnson, became famous for his trademark eyebrow raise and the tagline, "Do you smell what The Rock is cooking?" I wonder if anyone would have ever heard of "The Rock" (or pay money to go see his movies) if he had walked out and said, "Hi, I'm Dwayne, and I'm a wrestler. Thanks for your time."

Introductions are a critical component to making a lasting impact, both in wrestling and in the real world. They are one of the several unwritten rules of the game that take you from the bench and into the starting lineup; and we will cover a few of the most important ones in this chapter.

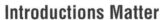

Introductions Matter

Maybe you're thinking, *"Well that's just great. Am I supposed to wear a leotard and jump on the tables to get noticed?"* While that *would* get you noticed, the point here is that in order to stand out, you can't sound like everyone else. If you want better results, then you first have to be just a little different. For most people, however, the formula for an introduction is pretty standard, which is why everyone's intro sounds identical to the person's before and after him. Here is a typical introduction:

> *"Yes, well, my name is Steven, and I just joined the organization. I came from ABC College, and I am, ah, just glad to be here."*

People smile at you, while simultaneously forgetting your name and anything else you just said. That's not how it has to be; but first that means you have to plan ahead and know what you are going to say before the meeting ever starts. Here is an example of a much better option:

> *"My name is Steven, and I am in the operations department. What brought me to ABC Company was my keen interest for helping achieve its aggressive expansion plans and my fascination with our company's unique culture that is filled with energy and opportunity."*

The real trick is to have your introduction prepared *before* your first meeting. The time to decide how you will introduce yourself is not as you are speaking!

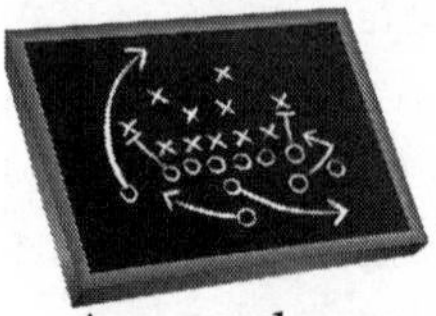

Take Control of Your Energy Level

As you learned in the previous chapter, overall energy level is an integral part of the company culture, which means that this particular aspect of your organization is essentially out of your control. What you can monitor and control, however, is your *own* energy level. And you need to, because it makes a huge difference in whether you are perceived as a real competitor or simply someone who is content to coast on the sidelines.

In my live classes, I make a distinction between 0%, 25%, 50%, 75%, 100%, and even 125% energy levels. What does this mean and why is it important? Your energy level, the level of enthusiasm and power you use to communicate with others, makes a big difference in how you come across.

I don't care whether you're an athlete, an art major, or a business major; you still have to deal with your franchise owner or coach, the owner of the art gallery, or the people in your organization. And no matter who you have to deal with, your energy level must convey the fact that you belong right where you are and you are committed to your role.

Your energy plays an important role in how you are perceived in much the same way your introduction does. And there are two key decisions you must make concerning your energy level and behavior before your first day at your new company:

1. **Decide to grow up.** Are you planning to behave at your new organization in the same manner you behaved in college? Determine what behavior and energy level you want to possess, and wherever you are today, start working toward displaying that in your everyday life as practice for the real world.

2. **Determine to get to the point.** You don't have to say a lot to stand out or get noticed. In fact, shorter and concise is always better than lengthy and confusing. Do you have a student in your class who just loves the sound of his or her own voice? It's the person who, when the professor calls on him, the rest of the class rolls their eyes and mumbles under their breath, "Oh no, here we go again." This person spouts off for a few minutes, and at the end of it all, you have no idea what was just said. Don't be that person. Determine to say what you have to say in a way that allows everyone to quickly get your drift but also to remember what you said.

So, how do you take control of your energy level? It's really pretty simple: *95% of the time, you can be exactly who you are, but the other 5% of the time, you need to step it up.* Most people act the same way 100% of the time. The supposed reasoning for this unwillingness to change is often something like, "I'm just being true to myself." *Yawn. Boring. Heard it all before.* That's not a reason—that's an excuse. People can change their behavior if they really want to without feeling like they aren't being "true" to themselves. Stepping up your game to stand out at your company does not require betraying your inner self. It simply requires a little dreaded four-letter word: WORK.

> The level of enthusiasm and power you use to communicate with others makes a big difference in how you come across.

Let's assume that in class, you consistently perform at about a 50% energy level, which probably comes across as monotone and forgettable, at best. This won't cut it in the real world. If you don't think you have what it takes to speak up during a presentation, think about the last sporting event you attended where you were cheering at the top of your voice or the last time you saw your best friend and were so excited. Were you not being you? I have no doubt you were being yourself—and I've just proven that you have the ability to raise your energy level and change your behavior from 50% to 100% when you feel like it. So, why not do it at work when it will benefit you the most? *I'm not even talking about all the time. I'm talking about being more alive, attentive, and alert a mere 5% of the time.*

If you go to a meeting and somebody asks you a question, everyone will judge you based on your response, whether you

"Normal" Isn't An Excuse

I was invited to speak to a group of twenty-five Japanese exchange students taking an ESL course at Highline College in Seattle. When I showed up on campus, the first thing the professor said to me was, "Just so you know, they're going to be kind of quiet." I already knew this—it's the "normal" Japanese behavior. But within five minutes, I had the entire class talking and asking questions. The professor was stunned. They were louder and more confident, all because I simply challenged them to take their 5% Zone out for a spin to see how it felt. One of the female students remarked, "Mr. Krempl, my English not so good. That's why I no ask questions."

Stephen: "Well, do you have a question now?"

Girl: "Yes."

Stephen: "Okay. Write it down."

Girl: "Now?"

Stephen: "Yes. Write it down now."

She wrote the question down and I said, "Okay. Now put your hand up and say, 'Mr. Krempl, I have a question.' Then, read it aloud." By writing it down, it took away the fear of mistranslating from Japanese in her head to English out loud.

By the end of the class, there was a line wrapped around the room waiting to speak to me, all because I showed them when to put aside their normal, comfortable behavior and find their 5% Zone in front of the most important audiences.

like it or not. If you are rambling on at 50% energy level, someone is sitting there thinking, "What the heck are you saying?" Don't let this happen to you. Instead, stand up with at least 75% energy level and think, *"This is an important meeting. It's time to be different from my normal 95% self. This is my 5% time, so I'm going to be a little louder and have more energy."* In the end, it's a deliberate choice, and you're the one with the power to choose.

Go Ahead, Decide to Stand Out

Whether you are quiet, painfully shy, or both, it doesn't matter. You can stand out as much as anyone else. It's a choice. I was invited to a lunch where the guest speaker was Karen Hughes, the vice-chairman of Burson and Marsteller, which is the largest consulting PR firm in the world. She was also one of George W. Bush's communications directors during his presidency. There were about 180 people in the room.

From the agenda, I knew there would be a Q&A time following her presentation, and I wanted to make sure I asked a good, standout question. So, I prepared a couple of questions (just to be on the safe side), and by the time she finished, I was ready. My hand shot up, but another guy beat me to it. I thought to myself, *"Shoot, I already missed the first opportunity to stand out!"* And then it happened again! Someone beat me to the punch; to add insult to injury, that person asked one of *my* questions. *This was getting frustrating.* I knew I had to do something really different to get attention.

I soon saw my chance. The way the Q&A time was set up, she'd point to a person with his or her hand raised, and a runner with a microphone would bring the microphone over. I waited until the runner was on the opposite side of the room and shot my hand up. She motioned to me, and I quickly yelled out at the top of my voice, "I do not need the microphone."

Everyone turned to look at me; that certainly got everyone's attention. Believe it or not, that wasn't easy for me, because most of the time I actually prefer to hide. It's not always easy to stand out and sometimes it requires a big leap outside your comfort zone. But in the most important situations, those 5% situations, you must find a way.

Not a Morning Person, Eh? Yes, it is always a conscious decision, even first thing in the morning. Let's say you don't believe you are a morning person and you often use an excuse to justify your sluggish behaviors in the early morning hours like, "I'm just not a morning person. I can't even function without my first cup of coffee."

Now, imagine you have a 7:00 a.m. flight you have to catch that morning, and you forgot to set your alarm. It's 6:15 a.m. What do you do?? You shoot out of bed in an instant! You go from 0 MPH to 125 MPH in less than two seconds. If you can do that, then why can't you also step it up at the next important 8:00 a.m. meeting? It's all in your head, and coffee (or any other excuse) is just a crutch that is holding you back from being a contender.

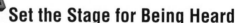

Set the Stage for Being Heard

Another thing related to energy is your volume. You need to know that in a small room, your voice should automatically go softer. In a bigger room, your voice needs to grow louder automatically to fill up the space. Volume control is a skill you need to master. You don't want to get caught mumbling or talking too loud—either way, it's distracting.

When it is your turn to speak and you've assessed what the best volume is to use, the next step is to summarize what you've heard, present your information with a stated purpose, and remember that shorter is better. Here is how to use "set up" statements:

- "I have one point to make…"
- "The key point here…"
- "What I'd like to add to these comments are two things..."

Using **set-up statements** lets your audience know that you have a point to what you are about to say and you plan to be brief and get right to it, which preconditions them to be more likely to actually listen to what you are saying. In my live classes, I give feedback to participants by rating them between 1 (not good) to 10 (very good). And then we work to ensure that everyone knows how to get to at least a 7.

Your boss is probably not going to give you feedback on your volume or the impact of your statements. Rarely will you hear, "Clarisse you're too soft. Can you speak at a 7? You're at a 3." Or, "You need to get to your point more quickly." But you know what? When it comes to promotion time, you boss will be sure to say, "Clarisse doesn't have the oomph to lead our group. She talks and talks but doesn't ever really say anything. Let's promote somebody else."

Be There When Your Name is Called

Organizations often have large functional meetings where they introduce the newcomers. If your company does this, it's important to be there when they call out your name. Here is one way the intro could go:

> *"We'd like to introduce those who have joined us in the last month. The first person is Ellen Smith. Ellen, are you with us today? Has anyone seen Ellen? No? Okay, moving on..."*

Ouch. That's one of the worst things that can happen, especially when you are new. When the professor calls your name during roll call and you're not there, that's one class. But this is your future we're talking about. What does it say about Ellen if they call her name and someone says, "She left" or "She's not here?" It says that she doesn't care and she's not committed. It doesn't matter what the legitimate reason was (and I'm sure there was one). She will not live that down for at least a couple of months, and more importantly, she missed an opportunity for some top executives to connect her name with her face.

If an Introverted Engineering PhD Can Do It...

Job interviews can be daunting tasks for introverts. I once had the opportunity to provide a bright PhD with some feedback on his interview skills. After about five minutes, he had gone from about a level 3 to a level 4, but that was it. I stopped him and said, "First, if you act like that, nobody's going to hire you when you go for an interview. Secondly, if you act like that, I won't hire you."

That woke him up. This guy was a smart dude! He was getting his PhD in Engineering. He decided to switch it on, and he went from a level 4 to a level 7. He finally figured it out; he wasn't even aware that his "normal" was so subdued. Three weeks later, he told my staff, "I used every tip Stephen gave me, and I got the job." If this guy can do it, then so can you.

The Devil's in the Details

In professional sports, athletes spend countless hours on the finer details of their game. From a backhand or overhead to a swing, a pass, or a dribble, it's the small things that you practice that make you great. The greatest players practice little things until they perfect them. It's this unspoken rule that separates the world-class athletes to the ones no one has ever heard of.

Big Money Speaker, author, and coach James Malinchak related a quote to me that Michael Jordan shared at one of his bootcamps: "I always practice the little things. It's a little dribble here or a small change to my jump there; and I keep doing it until I get it right." Well, if Michael Jordon does it, then how many times do you think you should practice the little things that make you stand out or connect with people in an organization? Practice, practice and more practice are the keys. The only way to improve, and ultimately, to stand out in the cutthroat professional work world, is to perfect the little things.

Content Versus Process. When it comes to the little things, there is an important differentiation I need to make. Let's say you are preparing a presentation. Do you think the most important details are what goes on the slides or what doesn't go on the slides? The answer lies in the difference between **content** and **process**. The *content* is everything on your slides or in your presentation. The *process* is everything you're going to say or do with the information you present. What questions do you ask about that slide? What stories are you going to tell to emphasize the content? Do you move or write a key point on the white board? What statements will drive home the most important points you want to make? And what activities do you want the audience to do to help reinforce the content? These are all the elements that comprise the process.

> Practice, practice, and practice—those are the three things that will help you stand out and connect in a lasting and powerful way.

As a general rule, the process is more important than the content (I assume you already have good content). Many of your professors may disagree with me, but it's true—especially in the real world. If you have really complex, in-depth slides, but I engage the audience better than you, I win. Let me repeat that. If your stuff looks great, but it doesn't resonate with the audience, while my audience leaves going "Wow! I learned so much!" then yes, I win.

Here's where most people go wrong when it comes to PowerPoint. They spend 98% of their time making their slides flashy. Stuff flies in, more stuff twirls out. Please just spare me. Yes, the look and design of your presentations matter, but the time you spend on the process is more important. If you spent even 50% of your time thinking about how to engage the audience, how to use appropriate set-up statements, and when to increase your energy level, you will win, hands down.

The best of the best practice the little things and focus on *process* over *content*. Even then, there are obstacles that stand in the way of your rise to the top. The following story demonstrates how the feelings of the majority can often keep you down:

You Can't Keep a Good Crab Down

In the Northeast United States, when crab fishermen catch their prey, they place them into shallow open boxes. The boxes are designed such that the crabs could literally crawl right out of the top. In many other countries in the world, they put crabs in deep baskets, and they bind their claws with rubber bands. Not in the Northeast. They leave them in shallow baskets with open claws.

Why don't the crabs just crawl right out? The reason is fascinating. When a crab feels another crab crawling over its back to escape, it reaches out and pulls the crab back down. It becomes a self-policing box, and the fishermen don't have to do squat. When one crab decides to make a break for it, the other crabs pull him back in.

So as it turns out, you *can* keep a good crab down.

Do you have friends who are crabs? If you say to them, "Hey I figured out how to do this…" the crabs are the ones who laugh and dismiss you with, "No, no, no. It won't work. I tried that before." The next time you feel someone trying to pull you down, just say, "Crab!" (I recommend doing this in your head only. Randomly yelling, "Crab!" is not a great way to stand out). They are simply trying to pull you down to their level. They don't know what you know. They haven't spent the time practicing. And if they can't succeed, they don't want you to either. Don't let those crabs pull you down.

The same thing happens in organizations. People who are survivors or cruisers will always tell the people who contribute and win, "Nah. Tried that. Doesn't work. Save your breath. Don't bother." But that's just not true. The survivors and the cruisers don't put in the effort that you are prepared to put in, but they still become jealous when you try to rise above. But rather than rise to the occasion and compete themselves, they're content just to hold you back. The choice you have to continue to make is this: *Will I stick with the crowd or instead teach them that there is another way?*

There are a lot of crabs around who are not prepared to put in the work that you do. It's no different from being a tennis or basketball star. If you're out there shooting hoops or practicing your serve for three hours after everyone else went home, the crabs won't like it. They'll scoff and say, "What are you doing? You're wasting your time. You're good already."

But the best don't want to be good. They want to be great.

If you're game, go to www.stephenkrempl.com/practice
to try out your skills.

Coach's Corner

Energy Level Awareness Practice

I'm going to show you how to raise your energy in one minute. In the time it takes to do this simple exercise, you will move from a 0 to 25 to 50 to 75 and 100% (and maybe even 125%) energy level:

1. Take a seat in a chair.
2. Let's start with 0% energy. How would you sit in the chair if you had zero energy? What does no energy look like and feel like to you? You are probably totally limp and slouched way down in the chair.
3. Now 25%. How would you sit in the chair at a 25% energy level? You sit up a little, but you're still overly relaxed and a bit slumped over.
4. Now take it to 50%. You are probably sitting up a little straighter in the chair with your hand on your knees. Your eyes are brighter and your head is level.
5. Let's go higher. Take it to 75% or 100% energy level. Is your back tall and straight with your head held high? You are engaged and leaning forward.

This exercise is the physical embodiment of what it means to change your energy level. It is a conscious decision to physically change your position and stance. Everything requires energy, and right now, you have a default energy level for everything you do. Whether you're standing up and speaking, sharing your point of view, or introducing yourself, you always have some level of energy. And once you recognize your own energy level, it will be easier to know how much you have to change it in those 5% moments.

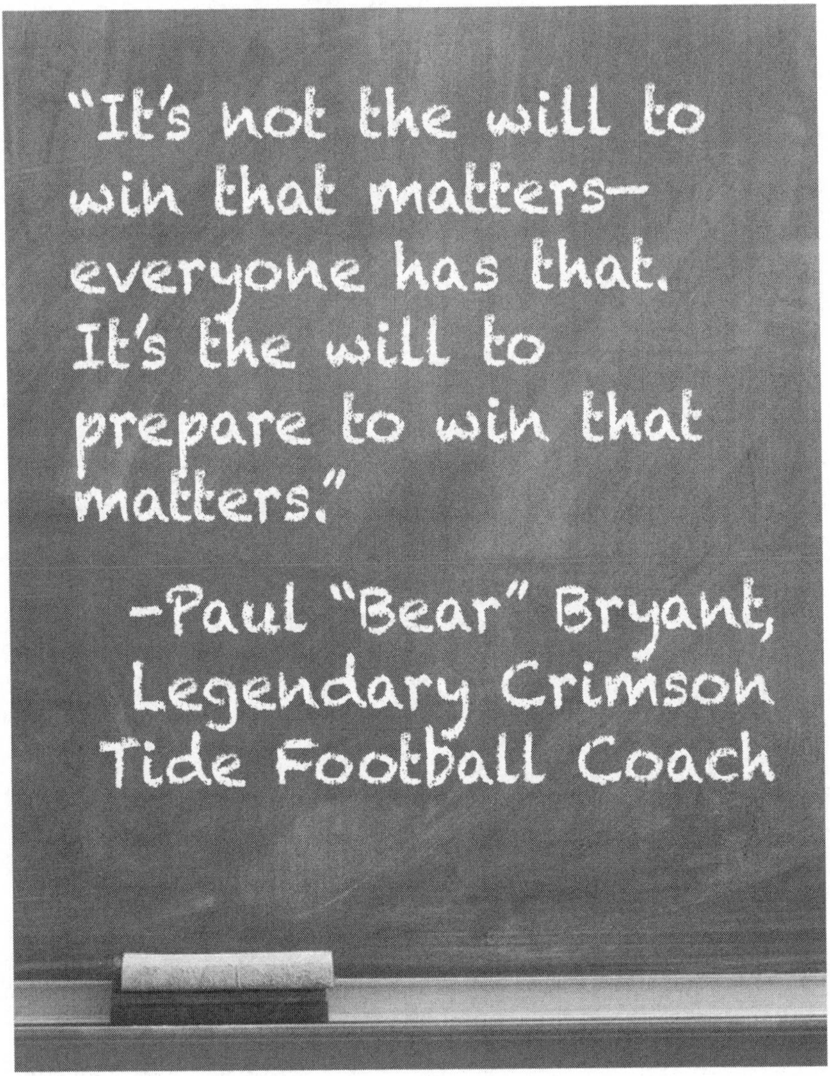
"It's not the will to
win that matters—
everyone has that.
It's the will to
prepare to win that
matters."
-Paul "Bear" Bryant,
Legendary Crimson
Tide Football Coach

Chapter 9

The Playing Field: Choosing the Right Company to Match Your Strengths

"Only you can determine the right playing field for your skill set and personality. It's certainly not 'one size fits all' when it comes to companies."

-Stephen Krempl

The very best athletes have an endless sea of options when it comes time for them to choose the right professional team. For example, an all-star college pitcher can have his pick of almost any franchise. He can choose a team with a well-known reputation and proven track record; or he can choose a smaller, newer team with more potential for growth and more flexibility. When it comes to the corporate playing field, you will also find a vast array of teams (or companies) from which to choose. And much like the different MLB team franchises, each type and size has its distinct advantages and disadvantages. This chapter will give you the information you need to decide what type of organization fits you and your needs.

Types of Enterprises

Enterprise—it's not just the name of the ship from *Star Trek*. The term enterprise is defined as any size business or company; but for anyone who knows anything about business, you know that there is a vast difference between a "Mom and Pop" coffee shop and a large company like Starbucks, just like there are no subtle dissimilarities between the corner store and a global giant like Wal-Mart—and yet they are all examples of enterprise.

Have you thought about what size company feels right for you and your skill set? To help you determine this, you must first know what your options are in the corporate playing field. Until about twenty years ago, the business world was divided into small, medium, and large companies. But with the explosive growth in the number of businesses, types, and sectors, the playing field has expanded a great deal. Nowadays, depending on whom you ask, you will get many different answers on what exactly constitutes the "size" of a business.

It used to be that one could define an organization in one of three ways: Number of employees, turnover, and balance sheet. But many now say that in the age of information, classifying the size of an organization by these criteria has become imprecise; and given the number of unofficial and official classifications out there today, it seems they are right. Here is a list of a few of the categories of business you may come across once you enter the playing field:[1]

- Start-up
- SOHO (Small Office/Home Office)
- VOHO (Virtual Office/Home Office)
- Micro business
- Small Business
- Lower mid-size Business
- Medium-sized Business
- Mid-Sized Business
- Upper mid-size Business
- Small-to-Medium Enterprise (SME)
- Lower Mid-Market
- Mid-Market
- Upper Mid-Market
- Medium-Large Business
- Large Enterprises

Got it? Me neither. The challenge is that there is little standardization around the common use of these terms. And however you want to categorize them, there is seemingly no end to the types and sizes of business today. So, for the sake of simplicity (and your sanity), we are going to refer to a company by its number of employees like you see on the following table:

Name	# Of Employees
Micro Enterprise	<5
Small Enterprise	<100
Small/Medium (SME)	< 500
Medium Enterprise	< 5,000
Large Enterprise	> 5,000

The ceiling or cap for the exact number of employees in each category will vary depending on whom you ask. But in terms of your understanding, we will discuss general sizes and what the various sizes mean to the company culture, and more importantly, to your career. Let's start with a quick look at micro businesses.

Micro Enterprises

In the United States, a micro enterprise (or microbusiness) is a type of small business with five or fewer employees. It's a term that has only been in wide use for about the last two decades. Many of these businesses actually have no employees other than the self-employed owners. In terms of resources, microenterprises generally need less than $35,000 in loan capital and do not have access to the conventional commercial banking sector.

Microbusinesses usually consist of people who work from home or have home offices where they work for themselves in some capacity. Chances are, you know several people who fit into this category, as it is growing in popularity by leaps and bounds each year, thanks in large part to greater access to business tools via technology and the Internet.

In his book, *Make Money with a Microbusiness*, author and microbusiness owner Anthony Hilb states that, "Microbusinesses have existed since people first exchanged goods and services in their communities. Today, microbusinesses can have a much larger impact; products and services can be exchanged at previously unimagined volumes, distances, and speeds. Credit here is due to advancements in technology. With the Internet, apps, and other technologies available (often for free), microbusinesses will continue to explode in popularity."

Small Enterprises and SME's

Over half of the enterprises in the United States are considered small to medium size with 500 or fewer employees. Small to medium-sized enterprises (commonly known as SME's) are most often privately owned and operated corporations or partnerships. Small businesses are also what you probably think of when you think of a neighborhood chain or a locally owned business. Typical examples include convenience stores, bakeries and restaurants, regional accounting or law firms, repair companies, hair salons, small-scale manufacturing, and online businesses, such as web design and programming.

Despite what you may think, small businesses are thought to create the most new jobs in communities. Not to mention the fact that local businesses provide competition to each other and also challenge the corporate giants. In short, small businesses are invaluable, and they keep the big guys on their toes!

Medium and Large Enterprises

A large enterprise is generally a company employing over 5,000 people, while a medium company can have anywhere from 1,000 to 5,000 employees. This size organization has grown to the point where it has several large national or international offices or headquarters with loads of dedicated, full-time staff to manage all the parts of the complex infrastructure. The medium and large enterprises are the ones you hear about most often, the ones found on lists like the *Fortune 500*; and most of the time, these companies are publicly owned (i.e. they have shares freely traded on a stock exchange).

Maybe you're thinking to yourself, "*Good to know. Now how does this affect me?*" On the surface, the category names and numbers themselves don't mean much. But once you start to work for any company, there are certain aspects of your job and your future at an organization that will be greatly determined by its size. In fact, there are some important pros and cons of working at both small and large enterprises that may be what you need to know to determine the best fit for you.

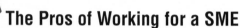

The Pros of Working for a SME

Like many college students, you may be drawn to the flash and allure of a large company and overlook the possibility of working for a small business. Working for a small business can be substantially different from working from a medium sized or large business in ways that many students don't realize. Here are a number of reasons to work for a small to medium-sized enterprise:[2]

Less Red Tape. Large companies need more standardized procedures to make sure that work is streamlined and employees receive fair and equal treatment. For example, if you work at a small business and you need a new laptop, you can ask your boss and he will probably say something like, "Ok, order one and send me the receipt. Oh, and keep it under $1,000." You won't get that kind of response at a large enterprise. If you need a new computer at a large company, you will have to fill out forms and likely wait for approval from multiple levels.

Less Orthodox Hiring Practices. While larger organizations rely on their reputation and a presence at graduate recruitment fairs, it is unlikely that smaller enterprises will rely on either. They may have to work a little harder to get your attention. In fact, some SME's are rather unorthodox in their approach to recruitment—if they meet you, like you, and see that you are a fit in their organization, they may have the freedom and ability to hire you on the spot. In some cases, it may be less about what your resume says and more about a personality fit.

More Casual Atmosphere. You will find a more relaxed dress code at many small businesses. When working in a non-traditional office setting, you might even be able to wear jeans to work. You're also more likely to be able to take breaks when you need them, eat snacks whenever you're hungry, and listen to music while you work.

Easier to Get Noticed. At a small enterprise, you are battling fewer people for the spotlight. And when you are more closely involved with your boss, it can be easier to justify raises and promotions because the person who can give you these things will have plenty of firsthand knowledge of what you've done for the company.

Learn From the Boss. In a large company, you may never interact with (or even meet) the CEO, but in a small business, you're more likely to interact with him or her frequently or even work directly for the owner or CEO.

More Responsibility. This one could probably be listed in the "cons" as well. When you work for a small company, there will be times when decision-making tasks will fall on you whether they are supposed to or not (and whether you want them to or not). You'll also quickly learn to handle the stress of decision-making and how to make the decisions that your boss wants you to make.

The Cons of Working for a SME

One of the biggest financial decisions that you will make in life is deciding where you want to work; and just like any business, there are some undeniable drawbacks to working for a small business that you need to consider:

Lower Pay. Many small businesses simply do not have the resources that large companies do. While you may gain more experience, you'll often get paid less than you would for the same work at a larger company. You're also unlikely to get as many benefits as a large company could offer.

Fewer Vacation Days. Small businesses have fewer employees, which means that there are fewer people around to pick up the slack when you're out. If vacation days are important to you, make sure to pick a boss who values his vacation time as much as you do and will encourage you to stay home and recover when you're sick.

Increased Workload. With more work and fewer employees to spread it around to, any increase in workload will frequently fall on you.

Less Opportunity to Meet New People. Large companies can be great places for making new friends. If you don't really click with the people in your department, you can always find some people in another department to have lunch with instead. If your company only has five employees and you don't get along with them, you're out of luck. Small companies can even be lonely at times, as there may be days when everyone is out except you.

More Menial Tasks. Small business may not have cleaning staff, suppliers, or dedicated receptionists. If you think that taking out the trash, doing the dishes, answering phones, opening mail, and making a supply run shouldn't be in the job description of someone with your degree, a small business may not suit you.

Limited Mobility. Particularly in well-established small companies and extremely small companies, job titles may be well filled or beyond your reach. If the only job titles in your company are President, Assistant, and Accountant, there isn't a lot of room to get promoted.

More Potential for Blame. Since you're likely to have greater responsibility in a small business setting, you're also more likely to be the one who gets blamed when things go wrong.

Lack of Name Recognition. In many fields, it doesn't matter if anyone has ever heard of your company or not, but in some fields, working for a company with a big name can be the key to your future success.

The Pros of Working for a Large Enterprise

It's important to know both the good and the bad before you commit to any workplace situation, especially since you're going to be spending the majority of your time there. So, now let's look at the pros and cons of working for a big business. We'll start with the pros:

Better Pay and Benefits. Larger companies can typically afford to offer their employees more in the way of compensation, and there are commonly better benefits packages, which can include things like healthcare, 401Ks, paid leave, stocks, and even education assistance.

More Opportunity for Advancement. There are more positions in a large company, which means more opportunities for you to get ahead. Also, access to top management positions is not limited by nepotism, as is often the case in smaller businesses.

A More Diverse Workplace. In a large company, there are more workers, which means you have an opportunity to network with a broader range of people, collaborate more often, and grow as a result.

More Perks. Big companies have lots of perks. They may have huge lunch facilities and high-tech sports gyms on their campus. Other perks may include company cars, expense accounts, and special "training" events in Hawaii or France, all at the company's expense.

Change Jobs Without Changing Companies. In a large enterprise, you can change your job—often multiple times—and stay within the company. If you decide you want to move from a development team, to a marketing group, to services, and back again, you can do it without having to update your resume and embark on a job search.

Better Name Recognition. When it comes to certain industries and careers, having the right name on your resume spells success, and a lot of time, that means the big guys.

The Cons of Working for a Large Enterprise

Each company has a culture, and the most successful employees conform to that culture. This can be a good thing; but for some, it means that a more rigid structure makes it harder to be seen (and heard) as an individual. Here are some of the biggest cons of working for a large enterprise:[3]

More Red Tape. The larger an enterprise, the more red tape there will be. As a result, projects move slower and taking personal initiative to get something done without getting prior authorization is typically out of the question. It's harder to reach decisions, and employees have less autonomy. You may have a brilliant idea, but by the time you follow all required processes, there's a good chance that it may not even resemble what you started with.

Getting Lost in the Crowd. In a large enterprise, it's more important than ever to practice ways to stand out, like the ones you have read about in this book. Otherwise, you're likely to become another name on the payroll.

Stifling the Entrepreneurial Spirit. If you have a more independent spirit, you may find a large corporate environment to be limiting or even boring at times. Because there are so many jobs within the company, you will probably be hired for a specific purpose, which may limit how interesting your job and your days are.

Dealing with Office Politics. Big companies are often criticized for having highly active office politics. If office politics are a turnoff for you or if you find them personally difficult to navigate, working within a large enterprise can be problematic. Certainly small companies can have office politics also, but as a whole, they tend to be less in smaller firms.

Top Concern is Shareholders (and Not You). Although not the case in many large enterprises, it is easy for larger companies to be more concerned about their public image or their stock prices than they are about your job satisfaction.

The Topic of Job Security

While many believe that careers at large companies inherently come with more job security, in the age of Enron, this statement is questionable. However, if you work for a company with one owner and five employees, and the owner suddenly dies of a heart attack, you're out of a job. It wouldn't happen like that at a large company because someone would be next in line to take over the boss's role, and the company and your job would remain intact.

But large companies, especially during the last few recessions, have been known to slash jobs by the hundreds or even thousands without warning. In short, there is no company or industry immune to job loss or uncertainty. Most of the time, it is a case-by-case thing. Research a company and its history so that you feel more secure about your choice. But you should always have a back up plan in place—because large or small, there are simply no guarantees.

Qualities Required by SME's

What skills are sought by SME's? The small and medium size enterprises seek the same skills as most employers, but in a smaller company some skills are particularly important, as you will need to use them constantly. Here are a few qualities that SME's look for in their employees:

- Ability to learn quickly but informally
- Self motivation and initiative
- Common-sense problem solving ability
- Ability to work with minimal supervision
- Flexibility
- Good communication skills
- Ability to work well under pressure

Qualities Required by Large Enterprises

All of the qualities from the list above are useful no matter where you work. But as you probably found when you considered both small and large colleges to attend, the large colleges are more "uniform" in their acceptance guidelines for students. The same is true for large enterprises—their requirements are often more clearly defined. The majority of large enterprises have uniform minimum requirements that MUST be on your resume for you to even get a second glance. In fact, most of them use advanced filtering software for incoming applications, which means that if your resume doesn't have the key words they are looking for, it will never even be seen by human eyes.

The key term for large enterprise is "transferable skills." Tangible and transferable skills are your tickets to a job at a big company. And once you have a list of the skills necessary to do the work, you'll want to match your skills and experiences to those that the company needs. What skills does the company want? These transferable skills will probably be the active verbs in the job description. For example, in the case of a business development job, it's likely they'll want somebody who can communicate, negotiate, manage relationships, lead teams, and strategize.

Only you can determine the right playing field for your skill set and personality. It's certainly not "one size fits all" when it comes to companies. Figure out what you enjoy most about big and small environments and imagine which one you would fit into the best. For additional help, use the *Coach's Corner* exercise on the next page to help you start to figure out the right direction to take.

Chapter 9 Footnotes

[1]Blackburn, Robert and Michael T. Schaper, Eds. *Government, SMEs and Entrepreneurship Development: Policy, Practice and Challenges.* London: Gower Pub Co, 2012.

[2]Cohen, Bryan. *How to Work for Yourself: 100 Ways to Make the Time, Energy and Priorities to Start a Business, Book or Blog.* Chicago: Bryan Cohen, 2013.

[3]Owens, Trevor and Obie Fernandez. *The Lean Enterprise: How Corporations Can Innovate Like Startups.* Hoboken: Wiley, 2014.

Coach's Corner

One Size Doesn't Fit All

Think back to your favorite classroom environments so far in college. Do you flourish in the large, auditorium style classrooms where you engage in large group discussions; and when necessary, you can "fly under the radar" without being noticed by the professor? Or do you most enjoy the classes with ten students or fewer, where a more intimate environment leads to more interaction and more frequent participation? In the end, there is no right or wrong way to feel about the size and environment of a classroom or a company.

Write down your favorite things about a small classroom environment and then about a small company:

Write down your favorite things about a large classroom environment and a large company:

Were you able to STAND OUT better in one of those environments? What can you learn from that and how might that affect how you act in your new job?

As you decide what road you will take, use this information and your personal preferences to guide your decision making process.

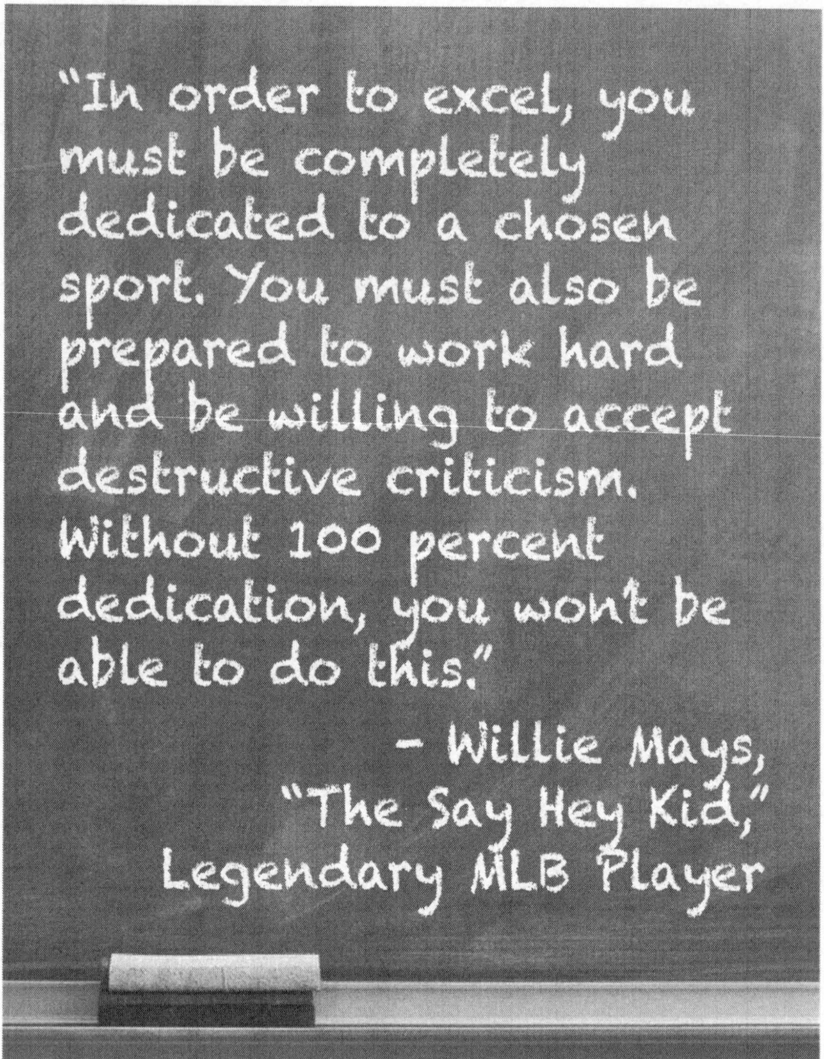
"In order to excel, you
must be completely
dedicated to a chosen
sport. You must also be
prepared to work hard
and be willing to accept
destructive criticism.
Without 100 percent
dedication, you wont be
able to do this."
- Willie Mays,
"The Say Hey Kid,"
Legendary MLB Player

Chapter 10

The Plays: Scenarios You May Face at the Office and How to Handle Them

"This is the stuff you won't find in any employee handbook."

-Stephen Krempl

It's the last six minutes of the championship game, and Tyler's team is in a jam. They've worked their hearts out and have played solid defense during the game; but the scoreboard always tells the real truth. They're two touchdowns behind, and if they don't step up their offense and be more proactive, they're going to lose. All the players are huddled around their fearless leader, looking to him for the next pivotal play. Tyler gathers his teammates in close and says, "Alright guys, let's get out there with no plan and just figure it out on the field. Ready, set, break!"

I doubt Tyler got many high fives after that game ended, and certainly no one poured the contents of the water cooler on him as they carried him off on their shoulders. No champion quarterback would head onto the field without contingency plans in place and active steps for winning. They know that if all they do is react to the other team's plays without solid plays of their own, they've got no chance to win, or even to compete.

There are many scenarios at work that everyone will face at some point in his or her career. And unfortunately, the improper handling of these situations can cost you the game, which may very well be a chance for a promotion, your reputation, or even your job. If you were playing a sport, you wouldn't get caught on the field without your next move. Why would you treat the business playing field any differently?

This is the stuff they don't tell you in orientation—and these are the scenarios you won't find in the employee handbook. No one else is learning this stuff before they step out onto the field, which means that you will have a huge advantage over the competition by learning these plays now. So, get ready for the plays by reading the following scenarios about real-life situations that you will likely encounter or need to prepare for during the early part of your career. We have categorized 27 situations into four categories. These are no means all the situations you will face, but they will definitely give you a head start:

- Personal Situations
- Situations with Supervisor or Senior Management
- Situations with Peers and Team Members
- Meetings, Projects and Other Work Situations

PART I: PERSONAL SITUATIONS

Scenario #1: Balancing Loyalty with Ambition

WHAT'S THE ISSUE? During his first week on the job, John was eager to learn everything and to know everyone in his department. He gave his opinion often and freely in discussions. He worked overtime and did excellent work. Everyone seemed to like him; but at times he did seem a bit too determined. When asked about John, one man who had been with the company for a long time commented, "You can't help but like John, but you can also tell that he'd abandon this department in a second if it meant getting closer to the top."

Erica started work on the same day as John did. Unlike John, however, Erica kept more to herself. She concentrated on her job and stayed in her area. She made an effort to learn from others and listened in order to understand situations before jumping in with suggestions. One of her co-workers said, "Erica is a really nice gal. I think she's going to make a strong employee. I like her." But Erica saw what a go-getter John seemed to be, and she began to worry that she didn't have what it took to stand out.

WHAT'S THE SOLUTION? Both John and Erica are off to a good start. In some environments, John would make more progress due to his outgoing attitude. In others, Erica would come out ahead. A lot of it depends on the overall culture of the company. Erica's attitude is definitely less threatening than John's.

In the long run, Erica may do better than John, because she is taking the time to develop stronger relationships with her co-workers; and loyalty is a critical attitude for others to sense in you. It's great to be ambitious, but it must be balanced with a caring, loyal attitude for the most success in the long run. One of the best ways to convey the fact that you are trustworthy and loyal is to make sure that you *listen* to the opinions of others instead of always pushing your own views.

Scenario #2: Impatient for a Promotion

WHAT'S THE ISSUE? Rosa feels really good about her new job; and so far, her supervisor seems happy with her performance. After four months, she's learned everything she needed to learn to perform her duties and is proving to be a good employee. Most people at the factory are close to one another and act like a family; but Rosa hasn't spent any time getting to know any of them since she has been spending all her time learning her new job.

Now that she can perform her job as well as or better than any of the other workers, lately Rosa's been thinking about becoming a supervisor at the factory. She figures that since the job comes so easy to her, she needs a new challenge. She makes an appointment with her supervisor to discuss what steps she would need to take in order to move up to a supervisory position.

WHAT'S THE SOLUTION? Rosa's performance got her off to a good start with the company. She has underestimated, however, all that it takes to be an *excellent* employee. In general, moving into a supervisory role requires that an employee has had excellent job performance over a *long* period of time. Rosa is simply unaware of all that it takes to become a supervisor. She should start spending more time getting to know her co-workers and supervisor rather than simply setting her sights on a fast promotion.

Scenario #3: Calling in Sick

WHAT'S THE ISSUE? After spending a great weekend camping, Kyle woke up Monday morning with a fever and a bad stomachache. He loved his new job, but realized that he would have to call in sick, and his co-workers would have to pitch in to do his work. As it turned out, staying home Monday wasn't enough. He also had to call in sick on Tuesday and Wednesday. Even after three days at home he still didn't feel well, but figured that he had better get back to work in order not to jeopardize his job. He went to work on Thursday and struggled through until the weekend.

The next Monday, Kyle was back to normal and everyone, including his supervisor, was glad to see him feeling better. That is, until Kyle started telling them about all the fun he had on his camping trip. He could talk of little else. He was so busy talking about his fun weekend that he forgot to thank his coworkers for covering for him. Soon he began to notice tension between himself and his co-workers. His supervisor also seemed more demanding.

WHAT'S THE SOLUTION? It might seem unfair, but being absent when you first start a job is generally more damaging than being absent later on. When Kyle, or anybody for that matter, starts a new job, he or she is still a big *question mark* in people's minds. New employees have not "paid their dues" yet. Kyle shouldn't have talked at length about his wonderful camping trip, and he made a big mistake when he didn't thank his co-workers for taking over his workload. Kyle's reputation has been damaged. It will take some time for him to be seen as a responsible person by others.

Scenario #4: Whom To Talk To

WHAT'S THE ISSUE? Bob seems to be burning your ears with gossip about the impending merger and layoffs that will follow. Bob is known to exaggerate a little, but he sounds so convincing and he has been at the company a while so he "knows stuff." You want to ask your supervisor about the rumors, but he is on a business trip, and you do not think that sending him an email is appropriate given the topic. But every day for a week, Bob continues to add fuel to the fire. And being new to the team, you are not sure whom to trust or believe.

WHAT'S THE SOLUTION? There are many Bobs out there, those who prey on newbies who will listen to their version of the truth. If you were thinking about going to your supervisor to clarify on the layoff stories, you are probably right to do so. But if he or she is not around, your next best option is to speak with someone in HR (Human Resources). You probably met someone who works in HR during orientation. That may be a good place to seek objective information if your supervisor is not there. Just swing by and ask, "Hey, I hear there has been some talk about layoffs…" There is no need to mention the source of this information, so be discreet about it and say, "I am new, so can you help shed any light on the rumors we're hearing?"

Scenario #5: Moving to a New Department

WHAT'S THE ISSUE? After six months on the job, Susan was called into her supervisor's office. She was relieved when Janet Lee asked her if she would like to take a higher profile role in another department. As it turned out, they had heard about Susan's excellent skills and work performance, which meant that Susan could have the new role if she wanted it. She is flattered, but at the same time she is not sure if she will get along with the staff in the other department. Susan had heard they could be a little difficult to work with and that the manager was rather demanding.

WHAT'S THE SOLUTION? Susan should get as much information as possible about the new department from Janet. Janet knows Susan's work and could possibly predict if she would be successful in the new department and if the new manager's style would suit her. If Susan decides that the opportunity for quick advancement is important to her, she should take the chance and learn to work with different bosses, which is an important skill for anyone's successful career.

Scenario #6: Remote Response Time

WHAT'S THE ISSUE? Pablo's morning commute has been pretty easy the last few weeks. He simply has to walk from his bedroom into his office in the adjoining room. Thanks to the nature of his latest project and the shortage of workspaces at his office, he has been working remotely. It's been great—for the most part. He's felt a little more stressed about the situation during the last week because his boss calls him to check in almost every hour. And when he doesn't answer the phone, it only seems to make the calls more frequent. He's starting to feel like his boss doesn't trust him, but he can't figure out why.

WHAT'S THE SOLUTION? In this day and age, there are more and more employees working remotely, thanks to the advances in technology. If you find yourself working from home or from a remote office like Pablo is, it can be tricky to determine exactly how rapid your response times need to be. Apparently Pablo's manager expects an immediate response from him; and since we don't know the manager personally, it's hard to know exactly why.

For many managers, quick and easy access to you is a clear sign that you're working, not watching *The Price Is Right* (which is their deepest fear). If Pablo happens to miss a call or IM from someone at work, he should simply reply as soon as possible. And more importantly, he does not need to offer a lot of excuses, but rather just explain what happened and get to the point with a simple, "I'm sorry; I was on another call," or "I stepped away for a moment. How can I help you?"

Scenario #7: Your Very First 5% Situation

WHAT'S THE ISSUE? It is Tammy's first day at work and her manager Neal says to the team, "Everyone, I'd like to introduce our newest member of the team Tammy Hall. Tammy, we are so glad to have you here. Now I will have everyone introduce themselves..." By the time it reaches Tammy, Neal says, "Ok, now tell us a little about yourself."

Tammy takes a deep breath and replies, "Ah... my name is Tammy, and I just graduated from college, and I really think this will be a great opportunity for me."

Then there is dead silence. Neal jumps in, "Well, okay Tammy. I am sure we will get to know you a little better as time goes on."

WHAT'S THE SOLUTION? In most organizations, staff is excited when new members join. This is because you are relieving someone from doing the job of two people, the department's workload has increased and you represent the help they need, or perhaps you bring some new specialty to the group. Whatever the reason, everyone is going to want to know a little about you. ***And on day one, you have the opportunity to climb on top of the rock or hide under it.*** The only way to be confident is to come prepared to share two or three things about you or perhaps even a story that shows you understand the culture, as discussed in chapter seven. Then people will think, "Wow, I better watch out for Tammy. She is such a confident, articulate and sharp person."

I know many of you could wing it—but you have the opportunity to make a great first impression; so why not prepare a little?

PART II: SITUATIONS WITH SUPERVISORS OR SENIOR MANAGEMENT

Scenario #8: Handling An Unexpected Job Assignment

WHAT'S THE ISSUE? Just before Tom went home on Friday after a month on the job, the manager informed him that she would be taking the next two weeks off, and she was appointing Tom to take lead on a project in her absence starting Monday.

Although Tom is the newest member of the team, he has the most knowledge on social media and is an excellent communicator. Tom doesn't feel confident that he will be able to handle the project in his boss's absence. He doesn't feel comfortable leading the meetings, directing the more senior team members, or handling conflicts that may arise between them. Tom feels that he will fail to adequately fill her shoes.

WHAT'S THE SOLUTION? Tom should call up his supervisor before she leaves for vacation and share his feelings with her. Perhaps she will be able to give some tips on dealing with certain individuals and reassure Tom that he will do just fine. Or even better, Tom could ask her for specific advice on how to handle the various scenarios that may arise during her absence for which he feels the least prepared.

Scenario #9: Unfair Workload

WHAT'S THE ISSUE? About two months ago, Amber's boss Mike came in with a simple request and a big smile. "Do you mind doing this extra report for me? Thanks! You're the best!" After that report, Mike gave her another one, and then another, and another, until now she is finding it difficult to get her own work done because she is so busy filing reports that are in Mike's job description. She is forced to stay late just to get her own required tasks completed. In short, she is completely overloaded with tasks that aren't in her work description, and she feels helpless to do anything about it. She might as well face it—she is the boss's new slave.

WHAT'S THE SOLUTION? Of course, most employees have a strong desire to please their superiors, and Amber is no different. But bosses aren't perfect, and there's nothing worse than having to take on two jobs but getting paid for only one. Sometimes, you just have to learn to say no. Amber needs to meet with Mike to review her work description, and if it becomes an ongoing problem, go to HR. As a worst-case scenario, she may need to transfer to another department (some people just won't change).

Scenario #10: Telling It Like It Is

WHAT'S THE ISSUE? Lately, Jim has been embellishing feedback that they have received from customer surveys. The higher-ups will undoubtedly receive his changes to the reports favorably, but Sandra knows this is not right, as things are not as rosy as the comments and data in the report are making them out to be. She has decided to go directly to the VP of their department and right Jim's wrongdoing before it's too late.

WHAT'S THE SOLUTION? When something in the workplace is awry, sometimes the first instinct is to take a complaint straight to the top. But corporate hierarchy is the name of the game in most companies, so if Sandra skips too many levels, she may end up aggravating many who work above her. She should take the complaint to her direct supervisor first, and address her complaint as a "concern" about the report findings. Remember that it's not always what you say, but also how you say it and to whom.

Scenario #11: When Do I Respond?

WHAT'S THE ISSUE? It is the end of the first week and your boss just sent you an email asking you to research some data that she needs for a presentation. But it is 5:00 p.m. on Friday, and you had planned to meet some college friends at 5:30 p.m. to celebrate your new job. As you contemplate what to do, you tell yourself, *"It's Friday afternoon, so she can't possibly need it now, right?"* You know it would take at least an hour's worth of work, maybe more. So you decide to reply early on Monday before 8.00 a.m.—and that should take care of it.

WHAT'S THE SOLUTION? Nobody likes to get an email or request to do something on Friday at 5:00 p.m. And in many cases, replying on Monday is acceptable. But what if your boss is in a time crunch or planning to work over the weekend on the task? That may mean that he or she is depending on getting the information from you in a timely manner. You want to get off on the right foot when you begin a new job, so the best thing to do is to swing by the supervisor's office and ask him or her when you need to have the information or task completed. You may find out it can wait, or you may discover that you need to push your drinks back an hour or so with your friends. That's a much better option than creating a bad impression at the beginning of your career.

Scenario #12: Just Show Up?

WHAT'S THE ISSUE? Bill just started his new job last week. Today, his supervisor's assistant sent out an email for everyone on Bill's team that said: "Steve is going to Washington, D.C. to make a presentation entitled, 'Developing an Innovation Culture: Our Experience' this Friday. He would like you to attend a short meeting to give him some feedback and suggestions to help enhance his presentation. Don't worry about it just show up." Bill shows up and soon realizes everyone has at least a couple of suggestions or comments that seem to have been well thought out, and some even brought relevant articles. But Bill could have sworn that the email said "just show up."

WHAT'S THE SOLUTION? When you receive a note that says "just show up," what you may have missed is the unwritten rule that says come prepared to share your POV and to add value. Bill's supervisor would not have asked for everyone to come in just to walk through his slides without getting some real suggestions on improvements or enhancements. Otherwise, why waste everyone's time? If your boss thinks it's important enough to call the meeting, then you better go prepared.

PART III: SITUATIONS WITH PEERS AND TEAM MEMBERS

Scenario #13: The Office Gossip

WHAT'S THE ISSUE? After orientation Susan felt excited about her new job, but when she got to her desk, she realized she was not fully prepared for her new role with its fast pace and pressure. The next morning while pouring a cup of coffee in the pantry, Susan met one of her co-workers called Sally. Sally chatted with her and offered to have lunch together. Susan was glad that Sally offered to have lunch with her.

During lunch, the conversation took a turn. Susan did not expect Sally to talk about their manager, John, and how he was in "hot soup" with his boss. Sally told her how John always spread rumors and was not to be trusted. She also mentioned how Penny was an alcoholic and Larry was a time watcher. Sally then asked Susan to join her for lunch again tomorrow to continue the "helpful discussion" about the others in the department.

WHAT'S THE SOLUTION? Participating in gossip may be tempting, but it's almost always ill advised. Susan should politely decline the offer for lunch to finish the discussion. If Susan becomes too close to Sally too fast, her co-workers may figure that Susan is just like Sally and may not want to associate with her at all. Susan's best bet is to get to know everyone initially on an equal basis. When someone tries to share office gossip with you, change the conversation, or simply tell the person that it is not in your nature to talk about others.

Scenario #14: When to Provide Feedback

WHAT'S THE ISSUE? Michelle was irritated that her co-worker Nancy got to give the presentation at their monthly department meeting about a project on which they both were working. Michelle had more information on the project and had more experience with presentations. She was secretly fuming as the meeting started. During the presentation, Michelle noticed that Nancy misspelled several words in the presentation.

Michelle decided to say something. "Uh, Nancy? Sorry to interrupt, but you know that *procession* is spelled with two S's right?" You could have heard a pin drop, and Nancy was clearly caught off guard. "Thank you," she replied with a little disgust. As the presentation continued, Michelle was proud that she spoke up about Nancy's error and was confident she added value to the presentation.

WHAT'S THE SOLUTION? It's really not appropriate to point out people's mistakes in the open, especially in front of other team members or your boss. When providing feedback, make sure you choose the right time and do it one-on-one. Michelle could have come up to Nancy afterwards and said, "Hey nice job! I wanted to let you know you had a couple of typos..." Making someone look bad for the sake of you being right is simply not a professional thing to do. So, you have to decide if that is how you want to come across to others in the organization or your team. Some people may do it to you, but you can rest assured knowing that they will be the ones who look unprofessional, and not you. Remember the information from earlier in the book on how to bring up a point of concern (POC) in an effective manner.

Scenario #15: A Co-Worker's Annoying Habit

WHAT'S THE ISSUE? Small habits can wreak major havoc on productivity, and Chip knows that all too well lately. He can't help but notice Jennifer's obsessive pen clicking, Will's tendency to play his music too loudly in his office, and Adam in the next cubicle chewing gum like a cow munching on grass. They may seem like small habits to some, but to Chip, they've become intolerable now that he's put up with them for eight hours or more on a daily basis. In fact, if Chips keeps his feelings inside any longer, he may just lose it.

WHAT'S THE SOLUTION? Before asking his co-workers to stop a certain behavior, Chip must make sure that he isn't guilty of something as annoying himself. Also, he can see what he can do to block out the annoying habits like invest in headphones or try to focus on something else. If he really can't put up with it, then he can politely ask his co-workers to refrain. Chip could tell them in a humble, non-confrontational way that he gets easily distracted, thereby placing any perceived fault at his own feet rather than at theirs.

Scenario #16: A Saboteur Among Us

WHAT'S THE ISSUE? Amy is not prone to suspicion, but something is not right in her office lately. She suspects someone in the office is working against her. During her last few performance reviews, her supervisor Karen has told her about a few "issues" that someone else has been reporting about her (all confidentially of course). None of the issues are based on any facts, and Amy feels that someone is simply trying to sabotage her chances for a promotion. Pretty soon, her paranoia gets the better of her, and she starts to suspect everyone in her department. She becomes withdrawn and defensive, and Amy begins actively planning to thwart the purported offender and then get even when she uncovers the culprit.

WHAT'S THE SOLUTION? The thing about truth is that it always comes out eventually. The best thing Amy could do is calmly refute the accusations, provide any proof she has to the contrary, and move on with her job duties. There will always be the occasional hyper-competitive co-worker, but most people are not out to get you. Once Amy recognizes that, half of her problem is gone. Dealing with the obnoxiously competitive worker can be accomplished by simply doing her assigned work the best she can. The only one who she is really competing against is her own self; and others will notice when she steps up her work goals and accomplishments without stepping over others or buying into the drama.

Scenario #17: Working with the Enemy

WHAT'S THE ISSUE? It's no secret that Jordan and Brad don't get along. But they've mastered the art of giving cordial head nods in the break room, and they know what routes each other takes to the parking lot and the elevator. It may not be perfect, but it's livable. Unfortunately, their worlds are about to collide in a more permanent way. Their supervisor needs them to work on a collaborative project for which he needs both of their specific skill sets. After he finds out, Brad goes home and complains to his wife, "I'm going to have to quit my job! If I'm in the same room with Jordan for more than an hour, I feel like punching him!"

WHAT'S THE SOLUTION? Group projects can be trying even when everyone gets along, so these two are in a bit of a predicament. In order for a group to work effectively, there needs to be a good mix of leadership, people willing to take direction, and so on. Most of the time, groups aren't formed on such a basis, so there will always be group members butting heads. And sometimes group disagreement can escalate to extreme levels.

Since Brad and Jordan know from beforehand that they cannot work well together (and that previous collaborations have failed), they should see if they can apportion certain tasks to each person, and then meet only to put the separate parts of the project together. It's not ideal, but it's better than both of them quitting, getting fired, or failing on the project miserably.

Scenario #18: Giving Recognition

WHAT'S THE ISSUE? Paul is known for running great meetings. And at the end of his meetings, he always recognizes the efforts of someone on the team and asks other team members to do the same. You feel a little hesitant to say anything because you are really not prepared or know what the best way is to recognize someone.

WHAT'S THE SOLUTION? At the end of many meetings, the person running it will say something like, "Does anyone have something to add?" Also, a meeting agenda will often include "AOB" (Any Other Business). This is where you, as the new person, can quickly earn some points by thanking one or several people who have helped you and give them public acknowledgement for their efforts. This will show that you have the ability to recognize other team members for what they have done for you. Doing this early shows that you are fitting in and able to acknowledge the contributions of others.

PART IV: MEETINGS, PROJECTS, AND OTHER WORK SITUATIONS

Scenario #19: Too Much to Drink

WHAT'S THE ISSUE? It's the company Christmas party, and Ryan decides he really wants to let loose and enjoy himself. There's a great band, great food, and plenty of drinks. After a few rounds of Karaoke, Ryan has already had four drinks. He decides one more ought to do it, but before he finishes the final drink, he knows he's had enough. Too bad it's too late. He's already offended his supervisor's wife, told a co-worker's secret (while holding the Karaoke microphone), and spilled a drink all over the executive assistant Stephanie with no apology.

WHAT'S THE SOLUTION? It seems Ryan thought that letting loose during the social event couldn't hurt. Well, he knows better now. People have gotten fired for incidents at company parties. A social event at work is never an "anything goes" situation, no matter how you perceive others are acting. Ryan shouldn't have let himself act so immaturely. There's no telling how long it will take for him to live that down.

Don't let that be you. Chances are, Ryan knew he wasn't a "good drunk" and was prone to act foolishly while under the influence. If you can't hold your alcohol, simply don't drink, or drink very slowly to remain aware of when you are nearing your limit—and then stop before you reach it.

Scenario #20: Surfing on Company Time

WHAT'S THE ISSUE? It's a slow day at the office. There are a few projects to attend to and a few emails from the boss in the inbox, but George is just not in the mood. He decides to take a quick break and surf the Internet. The company frowns on using work time to pursue non-work interests, but what could a few minutes hurt? He jumps onto Facebook and reads a few posts, and then heads over to ESPN.com to check out last night's scores. There, that was relaxing, and no harm was done.

The next day, George does it again after lunch, then again the next morning, and again at lunch the following day. Before long, he's checking Instagram, Twitter, and Facebook almost hourly. It all started innocently enough, but before he knows it, he's surfing as he would be surfing at home, sending private messages and watching the latest sports clips.

WHAT'S THE SOLUTION? Most employers understand the need to take a break, and it's probably okay that George's computer screen isn't reflecting his work assignments 100% of the time. Still, he knew that he should have kept personal Internet surfing to a minimum, but it's just so addictive you start surfing or chatting or watching.

As a general guideline, don't write emails that you wouldn't read to the whole office and stay off non-work-related social media sites. And whatever you do, keep it clean. If your grade school teacher would object to something you are looking at or sending, then it's probably not okay at work.

Scenario #21: Interoffice Romance Gone Bad

WHAT'S THE ISSUE? Jim and Clara met at orientation and got on really well together for about the first three months; and then one day they didn't get along so well anymore. Once the blissful work couple, they soon found themselves at odds and constantly bickering. They decided to break up; however, the situation remained tense, to say the least. It was several weeks after the breakup and things were still really awkward and even hostile at times. In fact, their team members were starting to feel like they needed to take sides.

WHAT'S THE SOLUTION? While it can be difficult to deny an obvious attraction or connection with a co-worker, most office relationships are simply not worth the drama that they can cause. I'm sure that Jim and Clara felt they had found "something special." After all, we all know plenty of couples that met at work. But it's not ideal, especially if you really like your job and the company. Next time, Jim and Clara should do their best not to get involved with someone at the office. If it does happen, then they need to be professional about it and hold off on the PDA until after hours.

If an office relationship dissolves, the most important thing is to not talk about it openly with others. Try to be civil during office hours. If you absolutely feel that you can no longer work with each other, one of you should ask your supervisor to be transferred to a different area of the office.

Scenario #22: Another Meeting?

WHAT'S THE ISSUE? Since Andy joined his new organization, there seems to be a never-ending stream of meetings to attend: Weekly update meetings, work group meetings, one-on-one meetings, meetings with his supervisor, functional meetings, all-hands meetings, brown bag lunches, all-company meetings, emergency budget meetings, vendor review meetings, customer visit meetings, product reviews, and introduction meetings. Andy keeps wondering when do people get work done if all they do is attend meetings? And it's not like these meetings are ever succinct. Most of them are an hour or longer. Since he is new, he decides it is okay not to participate (which would just add to the meeting length anyway), but rather just observe and listen. After all, he has little relevant background experience thus far compared to the others in attendance.

WHAT'S THE SOLUTION? Remember even in the early days of your career, you will be expected to contribute, add value, and participate in meetings. Being new is no excuse for not participating. Remember you have to get into your 5% Zone, especially for the more critical meetings. So, prepare for and participate in meetings. Everyone is watching the new person, so this is your chance to show what you are made of.

Scenario #23: Department Lunch

WHAT'S THE ISSUE? Since Peter is new and just joined the team, his supervisor has decided to organize a welcome lunch for him. They go to a local casual dining restaurant with everyone on the team. Everyone is talking amongst themselves in smaller groups of two or three seated at a long table for eighteen. Peter decides that since he doesn't really know anyone, he will politely eat his food rather than risk butting in on a conversation.

WHAT'S THE SOLUTION? A lunch is never a lunch, especially when your supervisor is present, let alone your whole team. As a working professional, you should be able to use the F.O.R.M. acronym to hold your own discussion at lunch (as a reminder, F.O.R.M. stands for talking about the topics of *Family*, *Organization*, *Recreation*, and *Message*). Keeping quiet when you are new is not the best strategy.

Scenario #24: Company Ball Game

WHAT'S THE ISSUE? It was the end of Connie's third week and she has planned to go out with a few old friends to catch up on Saturday. She'd actually had this weekend planned for months since a few of her college buddies will be in town this weekend only. In this week's weekly meeting, Connie's boss reminded the team of the interdepartmental volleyball competition on Saturday that will be followed by drinks. All company directors and managers will be attending. When her boss asks Connie if she will be coming, she politely informs him that she has a prior commitment.

WHAT'S THE SOLUTION? Yes, Connie may have a prior appointment but consider the importance of such an event. Company socials are ideal informal situations to network and get to know more people and for them to get to know you. It is one of the best ways to talk to and interact in a less formal environment. When possible, you need to increase your visibility with people beyond your team. Connie's friends (and your friends) are important; however remember this—you will be at that company for the next few years and maybe longer. Your absence will be noticed, so make the call wisely.

Scenario #25: The Cupcakes

WHAT'S THE ISSUE? Jimmy is celebrating his one-year anniversary at the company. You found out about it because Jimmy had bought everyone cupcakes and put them in the pantry with a sign that read "Happy Anniversary Jimmy." Then he called everyone in and thanked the team for the last year and the support he has gotten. You heard later that your supervisor Mary did not condone to the "show" put on by Jimmy. You thought it was kind of cute.

WHAT'S THE SOLUTION? Every company and department has its own way of celebrating someone's birthday or anniversary. It is usually part of a standard ritual that is conducted at monthly or weekly meetings, where individuals whose special day has come are recognized. Depending on the company, the department may have a small celebration that could include a cake, meal, or gift. But it is unusual for a person to be the one to celebrate his or her anniversary. If Jimmy wanted to do that, he probably should have cleared it with his supervisor first to see if it would be appropriate.

Scenario #26: Volunteering

WHAT'S THE ISSUE? Josh's manager, Pauline, just announced at the end of the monthly meeting, "We need two volunteers to help organize the holiday party from our department. Any volunteers?" Everyone suddenly looks down at their notes, checks their phones for messages, and a few even get some "important" calls that they have to excuse themselves to take. Because there are no volunteers, Pauline says, "Okay, I want you to think about it and let me know at the next meeting, Otherwise, I will pick two myself."

WHAT'S THE SOLUTION? If you are new, you should be jumping at the opportunity to volunteer to help organize the next company social. You may not like it or think it may be a distraction, but it will help you get noticed and will also be a great way to meet and work with people from other departments. Not to mention you will make your manager's life easier if no one wants to volunteer.

Everyone has to do it some time or another. Get your time in early in your tenure and people will love you for it. Use it to your professional advantage because in many cases, the chairperson of such an event is someone senior, and it would be advantageous to get on his or her good side.

Scenario #27: Visitor's Impressions

WHAT'S THE ISSUE? Tom's manager drops in at his cubical and says, "Hey Tom, do you mind taking our visitor from corporate HQ out for lunch? Oh, and bring the new hire, Sally, along too."

Tom replies, "Sure. Who is this visitor?"

His manager replies, "Just the VP of Supply Chain. I am double booked, so if you take him out for lunch I would greatly appreciate it." At lunch Tom uses F.O.R.M. to talk to the VP, while Sally sits silently listening. After lunch, the VP says to Tom's manager, "Tom is really sharp. You must feel lucky to have him on your team." He doesn't even mention Sally.

WHAT'S THE SOLUTION? A lunch is never a lunch. How you come across and are able to carry on a conversation about work and other topics of interest to the other party will set you apart. Remember, people like to talk about things they are interested in, and you have to be interested in what they have to say in order to carry on a conversation. So, if you can be genuinely interested and also show an interesting side of yourself, you will leave a lasting impression. Learn this skill now because you will need to use it for the rest of your life if you want to stand out.

If you are about to step into an arena or a stadium to play a big game, chances are your coach has prepared you and your team for almost any potential game-time scenario. After all, that's what a playbook is for—to have practiced and ready responses for whatever may come your way. There will be an almost endless number of situations you will face during your career. That's just part of the game. But thinking through them and planning the best response BEFORE they take place will give you the competitive advantage you need to stand out from the crowd.

Some of the scenarios in this chapter were based in part on the following:

[1]Bishop, Russell. Workarounds That Work: How to Conquer Anything That Stands in Your Way at Work. New York: McGraw Hill, 2011.

[2]Hegar, Kathryn. Modern Human Relations at Work. Stamford: Cengage Learning, 2011.

[3]http://www.workhappynow.com/2010/03/16-difficult-office-situations/

[4]http://www.literacynet.org/icans/chapter07/six.html

[5]http://www.fastcompany.com/1795103/will-working-remotely-work-7-what-if-scenarios-consider-first

Coach's Corner

Make the Most of the Tools At Your Disposal

Although the real world is different from your college classes in many ways, you can still use your daily experiences to prepare for certain situations you will face once you enter the big leagues. For example, think back on your last semester of school. Were there any personality clashes with other students in your classes? What about with your professors? Chances are, there was at least one fellow student or professor with whom you didn't see eye to eye, and it may have affected you in one or more ways, such as the quality of class participation, the level of project involvement, or even your final grade.

The lack of communication is the cause of a multitude of problems in the real world like the inability to get along with co-workers or your supervisor and a general lack of connection to the company and the team. But if you can use your experiences in college as learning tools, you will have an edge over the competition and learn how to STAND OUT.

Think of one personality that rubbed you the wrong way in class. How did you handle interactions with that person? Did you talk over him or her or try to interrupt him or her?

How could you have handled your interactions better with a professor who was difficult to please or hard to read? How does this relate to your current job?

Think back to a time when a group or professor asked for a volunteer to head a project or activity. Did you step up? Why or why not? If you could do it over again, would you decide to step up and volunteer? Be aware of how you are/will react to such requests, as we normally fall into predictable behavior patterns.

____

____

____

Now think about a time when another student or co-worker was saying negative things about another person, a boss, or a professor. Did anyone stand up to this naysayer, or was this person allowed to simply keep spreading his or her negativity? How did you react? Did you jump in and add to the "stories?" (Be careful what you do in the organization, no matter how tempting it is.)

____

____

____

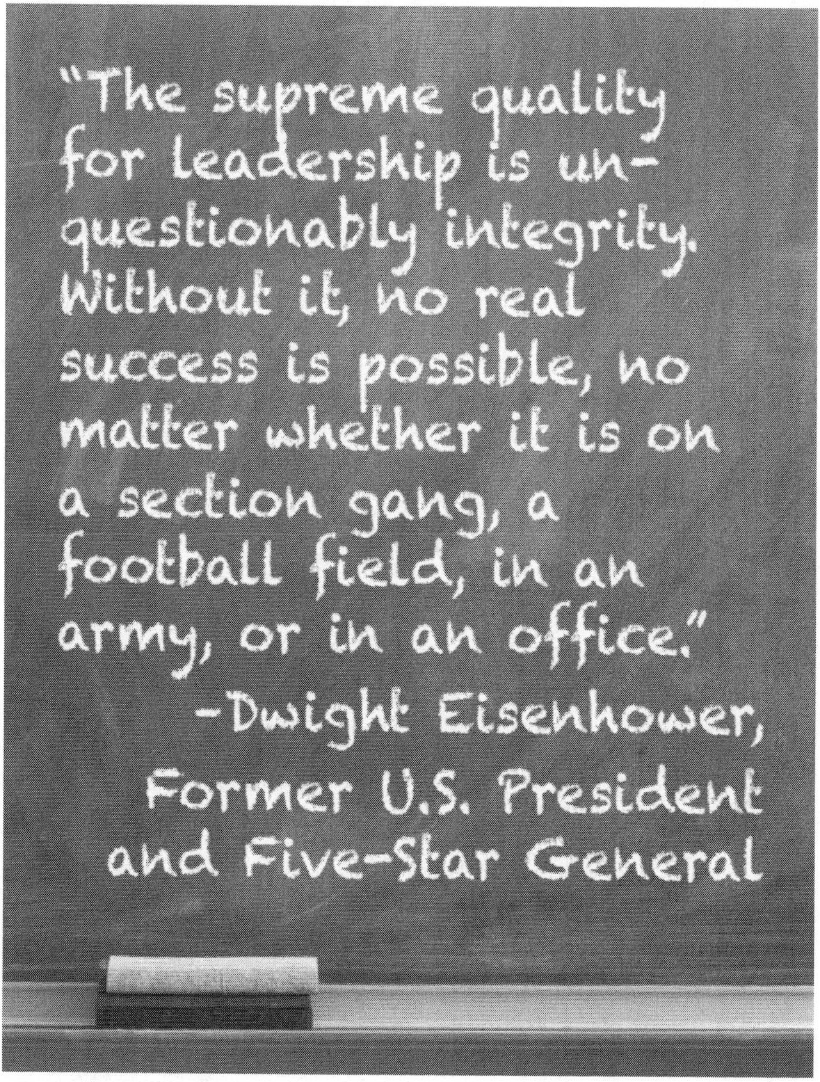
"The supreme quality for leadership is unquestionably integrity. Without it, no real success is possible, no matter whether it is on a section gang, a football field, in an army, or in an office."
-Dwight Eisenhower, Former U.S. President and Five-Star General

Chapter 11

The Officials: How to Get Noticed by Your Bosses and Superiors

> *"Place yourself in the position of partner, a valued person who helps solve problems, rather than subordinate, and you will solidify your importance to the company."*
>
> -Stephen Krempl

The officials of the game—some may argue that they are every bit as important as the players themselves. If a coach doesn't like a player's attitude or wants to "punish" him for something he did on or off the field, he can choose to bench him for one game or for the entire season. And we've all heard horror stories about referees who called games unfairly because of a bias, a personal preference, or a vendetta against a player, coach, or team.

Your interactions with the coach (your boss) and the referees (other leaders in the organization and the industry) really do matter—and there's no getting around that fact. So, rather than protest this truth, you should instead learn how to use it to your advantage. In this chapter, you will gain some valuable insight into the many different kinds of bosses—information that will be priceless come game time. You will also learn how to influence your boss, get your ideas heard and respected, turn your boss into your greatest ally, and in short, stay off the bench and in the game.

Know Your Boss

Many bosses, by virtue of their place of authority over their teams, come to believe that it's their way or the highway. So, as an employee who wants your own ideas to be heard and utilized, what can you do? And for that matter, how can you be sure you will get noticed by your boss and stand out for promotions and raises without being labeled as a suck-up or without "selling your soul" to get ahead?

While there is no secret formula for success, there *are* specific ways to influence your boss that will win you favor and keep you fresh in his mind as all-star asset on his team. Knowing how to influence your boss will make your workdays more pleasant and productive, not to mention you'll be at the top of the list when it comes to raises and promotions. There are a few basic guidelines to do this successfully without looking like a teacher's pet, a weakling, or disloyal to the rest of your team:[1]

1. Know What The Boss Likes. The best bosses know how to see past their own quirks, but there's a strong chance you won't always work for a boss who succeeds in that area. So, when you arrive at the office, take special note of your boss' hang-ups and peculiarities during the first few weeks. That way, you'll know which issues to stay away from and what you might not be able to change. Likewise, knowing what your boss likes can give you a foundation on which to build your ideas and proposals.

Decide today to view your boss as your partner, and not the enemy.

2. Prepare Religiously. In chapter five, we discussed the importance of being prepared. When it comes to impressing your boss and flying *above* the radar, it's important to have your ideas or third party validation information ready for the ideas you want to bring up. When you give a proposal to your boss, be sure you are able to justify why you think your ideas are viable and have facts to back them up.

3. Get to the Point Quickly. When you discuss your ideas, get to the point and be clear and concise. To ensure you do this, use setup statements to help you frame your responses and get to your points quickly. This will show that not only are you smart, but also you value your boss' time as much as you value your own. You also have to be crystal clear on the point you are trying to make. Wasting your boss' time is a quick way to get him or her annoyed; so present your case in a simple, easy-to-follow manner, and your boss will be more likely to listen to what you have to say or contribute.[2]

4. Be Realistic. Understand we all have our own pressures, problems, and stuff—and your boss is no different. In fact, you must realize the higher up you are in the organization, the higher the stakes and the more pressing the issues and problems become. Your boss is working with limited time and has concerns about which you probably are not even aware. So, treat your boss the same way you'd like to be treated. Accept that you are not going to change your boss's nature. Small changes in behavior are possible, but even those require considerable commitment.

5. Choose Your Battles. Not every argument is worth having or winning. If you think you are busy, imagine what it's like to do your job AND manage a team AND deal with a boss of their own. Remember that every request you make or discussion you start uses up some of his or her valuable time—so make them count.

6. Seize Opportunities. Take advantage of the openings you are given. Bosses who say they welcome emails should get emails. If they say they have an open door policy, then get inside their door. Those who ask for questions at the end of presentations should get questions from you, whether you are an introvert, think you are too new, or believe you can't yet contribute. Prepare your questions ahead of time (prepare religiously) and then keep your questions in a file on your phone so you will have them with you at all times.

Notice that "Flatter the Boss" did not make the list of strategies. Telling your boss how well he or she is doing, even if you think the opposite, is transparent and useless, and it will not win you a promotion or a bigger salary. All it really does is show that you have little to no self-respect. Plus, people can always see through insincere comments.

Becoming a Partner to your Boss

Building a better working relationship with your boss through these various strategies can unlock a variety of future possibilities, from promotions to easier interactions and bigger bonuses. In some cases, your chances for future advancement may be improved by helping the boss become more effective with his or her own bosses. Your boss's effectiveness relies on you and the rest of the team, which is why it's an unwritten part of your job to make the boss a better manager. Of course, the only way you can make someone else's tasks or job better is to first build your own career on a strong foundation that is characterized by a great attitude, competence and knowledge.

In order to become a partner to your boss, you have to change the way your boss sees you. You want him or her to see you as a partner, a "go to" source, and the one who gets things done, not a subordinate. By positioning yourself as a partner and a "go to" source, you can find new ways to connect with a boss that won't listen, remains distant or seems unfriendly. Partnering also offers a way to effectively deal with a boss who doesn't do his or her job well enough, who is overly helpful, or who is simply preoccupied. And it makes disagreements more manageable as well.

You have to understand that you are not the only one who will benefit from this shift. Your boss and your organization will benefit because both need your input, knowledge and expertise in order to succeed. Your boss isn't omniscient, which means you have to let the boss know the best way to manage you so that you can achieve your potential. Never fall into the trap of thinking, "Oh, my work will speak for itself."

While your boss will still be "the boss" no matter how much you convey a sense of partnership, this mental shift allows for a sense of collaboration over order taking. When you are the boss' partner, you are an ally in his corner, which means you won't stand by as your boss makes a costly blunder, overlooks important opportunities, or misses vital information when you can prevent it from happening. Of course, this assumes a high level of maturity that maybe you don't have yet, but it's never too early to start. So, how do you go from an "employee" to a "partner" in the eyes of your boss? Use a four-step process called **The Partnership Formula:**

1. **Change Your Mindset**. See the boss as a potential ally and a partner and start finding ways to solve the boss's problems or company problems.
2. **Be Understanding.** Make sure you understand the boss's world and what his biggest problems really are.
3. **Be Aware.** Be aware of the resources you already have or can learn and how to leverage them to your advantage.
4. **Pay Attention.** Pay attention to how the boss likes things to get done.

Tyrant or Difficult Bosses Demystified. If you have worked as an intern, had a summer job, or have worked while at college, you are likely aware that tyrant bosses are not just found in movies. And while most bosses are not dictators, they really do exist, so you better know how to deal with one in case you find yourself working for a tyrant or difficult boss one day. Let's look at one of the most famous "tyrant" bosses in the world, Donald Trump. How in the world would you navigate a workplace with "The Donald" as your boss? [3]

Before you assume that the correct answer is, "Don't piss him off and just do your job" there is actually a more constructive solution. Before writing him off as totally impossible to reach, assume that he might be a potential ally, which means that even Mr. Trump can be seen as a partner who is just as concerned about success and deeply worried about failure as you are. So, using the four steps from the Partnership Formula, let's figure out how to deal with a difficult or tyrant boss:

1. **Change Your Mindset.** First, change your mindset so that you see him as a potential ally, which requires a mental shift from being on guard or even scared in his presence to attempting to figure out what's behind all that bravado.

2. **Be Understanding** Second, you must try to understand his world. The "view from the top" is more cutthroat than you can probably imagine. In Trump's world, he needs to know his people are the best at what they do, and that they're savvy, skillful dealmakers.

3. **Be Aware** Third, become aware of what you bring to the table (or boardroom in this case). Are you most confident in your analytical thoroughness, your tough-mindedness, or your ability to hunt down deals like a pro?

4. **Pay Attention** Once you figure out what abilities most appeal to Mr. Tyrant, then step four is to pay attention to his needs so you can relate to his most common issues. Here is an example of what that might sound like:

"Mr. Tyrant, I am as determined as you are to find great solutions to our customer problems and protect our market share. I will work long hours and I'm ready to work longer if needed. You have years of experience in the industry, so when I do something wrong, please let me know how to do it better. I want to learn, and am open to direct feedback because it will help both of us."

Tyrant bosses are often just misunderstood. Whether your boss is quiet and reserved, shouting and overbearing, or somewhere in between, when it comes to all personality types, the key is to relate to them and what matters most to their own preferences and interests. [4]

Getting Your Ideas Accepted

Becoming the boss's partner isn't always easy. It's not uncommon for a boss to resist a subordinate's suggestions and ideas to improve working conditions or performance in his or her unit. Here's what the problem may sound like from an employee's perspective:

"I have great ideas for improving things, but my manager won't listen to any of them. When he does listen, he's quick to tell me why the ideas are bad or not worth the trouble. If he doesn't change soon, I'm going to transfer or just quit."

There could be several issues at play in this case. The boss may be a tyrant; he may be hardheaded; he may not be the best listener; or he could be all of those things. But if the boss is unwilling to listen to *anything* you have to say, there's a chance that the way you are communicating your ideas is contributing to the issue. So you have to stop and ask yourself a few questions:

- Are my ideas well thought-out and supported by facts? Did I prepare enough?
- How did I present my ideas? Did they address my manager's biggest problems and or concerns?
- Are my boss's responses really just a reflection of his communication style?
- Is the boss snubbing my ideas or just looking to find out more?
- Does my manager like fully developed ideas or to have his input early before the ideas are fully fleshed out?

Let's say you've explored all of these questions, and your boss is still resistant to your ideas. Here are a few other suggestions to keep in mind:

- **Are You Looking Out for Their Interest or Yours?** Whose interests are you really serving? Are you presenting ideas that help only you, or will they help your boss and the department as well?
- **Pay Attention to their Point of View.** Have you taken the time to understand the boss's world? Is your boss feeling overloaded and out of control? If your discussions represent more work for him, he may be reacting to that, not the idea.
- **Consider Their Recent Past.** Maybe your boss has been burned recently. It could be that his own boss is hard on his ideas. Or perhaps he was burned from another idea that went wrong in the recent past.
- **Lighten Their Load.** If your boss is overloaded, find ways to lighten his load. In other words, what can you do to help? If you think like an influential partner and not a lowly subordinate, then you'll want to find ways to help.

How To Share Your Point of Concern

It's one thing to present ideas that will help your boss or the company, but it's another to willingly cause dissent; so you have to learn the skill of disagreeing without being disagreeable. And it's especially tough to disagree with the boss without seeming out of line. Some managers are impervious to almost any kind of objection from subordinates, even though this may hurt their bottom line. Many people assume the worst about their bosses and decide that the boss is a negative, impossible person, and therefore steer clear. But by conveying a sense of partnership and continuing to communicate that you are on the boss' side, you can make an ally for life. So find out the best ways for your boss to accept differing points of view from his own.

One of the areas in which it is most desirable to influence managers is their ability to do their own jobs better so that you can do your own job better. Many people have decent relationships with their bosses and are satisfied with their jobs but see that their performance could improve if they could influence the way their bosses function. Nothing is more frustrating than to watch your boss do something poorly that you could help with but not know how without generating resentment.

Your boss needs to hear your POC, which means that you must learn how to disagree without being disagreeable.

As your boss's partner, you have an obligation to be forthcoming when you have information that could help. For example, you may know how the boss is seen further down in the organization and possibly by some of his or her colleagues and superiors. In addition, you may have some skills that your boss does not possess. Knowledge in these areas can be invaluable to a manager.

Part of why it is "lonely at the top" is because so few subordinates see that bosses need to learn and grow as much as their team members do. Good bosses appreciate the person who is willing to be helpful. The exchange of information about performance (or advice on how to improve it), in return for appreciation from the boss is a beneficial exchange that is too seldom executed.[5]

Get Their Defenses Down. One helpful way to disagree without being disagreeable is to lessen the blow of dissent with a little preparation. Here are the steps for lowering their guard:

1. First of all, begin the conversation by pointing out what aspects of a current strategy you believe are strong—and make sure you really mean it.
2. Next, you transition by saying, "But many of us are worried about…" The "many of us" helps because if your boss believes that the entire team feels a certain way, he is more likely to listen.
3. Then state your suggested solution, and don't just use some generic solution. Offer one that will work and explain WHY.

Ultimately, remember there is only so much you can do, so don't expect to succeed every time. Sometimes our efforts get through and sometimes they do not. But you still have to keep trying.

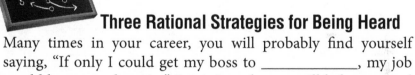

Three Rational Strategies for Being Heard

Many times in your career, you will probably find yourself saying, "If only I could get my boss to ____________, my job would be so much easier." Sometimes bosses will help you, and sometimes they will hinder you. That's just the way it is. The way to lessen the times that they become a hindrance is to learn the art of influence. ***Influence*** is really just the ability to get others to do things without force or coercion. Here are a few final tips for influencing your boss without seeming pushy, whiny, or needy:

1. Give Logical Reasons. If you need to make a request, always err on the side of more detail than not enough. Specific, well-thought-out reasoning will always win over vague and unplanned. Let's look at an example of what happens when you don't do it this way:

Tom: We need to update the workstations in our department.

His Boss: Okay, why? And how much money will it save us?"

Tom: I don't know. I'm not sure it will save us any money.

His Boss: Hmm all right. Then how much revenue will it generate?

Tom: I don't think it will generate any additional revenue.

His Boss: Okay, I'm not sure I'm following you here. Tell me again why I should invest the money to update the workstations.

Tom: We would be able to do a lot more things and we would be more efficient.

Yuck. That is the definition of a vague and general reason. To persuade and influence, you need data, facts, tangible cost reductions, proof of added value, and other believable information.

2. Give an Inspirational Appeal. There are times when appealing to an individual's need to serve a worthy mission may be a good way to influence without being overbearing. Appeal to individuals to do things because they serve a worthy mission. Show how the customers, owners, and employees will benefit. Explain how it will improve humankind. Just doing the right thing is a significant persuader for many people. Of course, to be effective, the appeal must be honest. [6]

3. Get a Second Opinion. Rather than merely request or demand something, check with others about their opinions. In the corporate world, this is called "socializing" an idea. Seek alternatives by asking people what they think. Present a thought and ask for improvements. People are much more cooperative on endeavors they help design. Do not ask for others' suggestions unless you are willing to listen with an open mind. And know that these appeals will not turn self-serving, arrogant, uncooperative individuals into smiling and obliging team players. Further, the use of these tools does not guarantee that you always get your way, but they do increase your odds of getting your ideas adopted if you can disclose with whom you have talked to about your idea.[7]

In business, the coaches (your bosses) the team owners (the top executives), and the referees (the other influencers) may look like they are calling the shots. And much of the time, they are. But that doesn't mean that you have to stand on the sidelines and never let your voice be heard. By positioning yourself as their "assistant coach" and exercising healthy influence methods, you will get more game time and stand out from the competition.

Chapter 11 Footnotes

[1]Greenberger, Leonard. *What to Say When Things Get Tough: Business Communication Strategies for Winning People Over When They're Angry, Worried and Suspicious of Everything You Say*. New York: McGraw Hill, 2013.

[2]www.ehow.com/how_2120968_influence-boss.html

[3]www.babsoninsight.com/contentmgr/showdetails.php/id/820

[4]Rao, Kathleen. *My Boss is a Jerk: How to Survive & Thrive in a Difficult Work Environment under the Control of a Tyrant Boss*, 2013.

[5]www.babsoninsight.com/contentmgr/showdetails.php/id/820

[6]www.wichita.bizjournals.com/wichita/stories/2005/12/26/smallb1.html

[7]Durre, Linda. *Surviving the Toxic Workplace: Protect Yourself Against Coworkers, Bosses, and Work Environments That Poison Your Day*. New York: McGraw Hill, 2010.

Coach's Corner

What Kind of Boss Will You Be?

By reading this playbook, you are already displaying the kind of initiative and "outside the box" thinking that makes for a great boss. And although that time may be a few years in the making, it's never too early to start figuring out what kind of boss you want to be. And before you say, "a great one" you need to examine what qualities and personality quirks you already possess. Because part of what makes up the kind of boss you are is not only your desire, but also your inherent qualities. So, based on the list of bosses on the previous pages, what boss do you most closely resemble in your life so far (although probably in a much less extreme form):

What traits do you possess that will make you a "Great Boss?"

What areas need the most work before you can become the kind of boss that even you'd like to have some day?

BONUS SECTION

Types of Bosses

The techniques presented in this chapter are effective no matter what kind of coach (boss) you have. And if there's one thing you can guarantee about your boss, it's that you can never guarantee what kind of boss you'll have. Just as all of your friends and classmates have different personalities, strengths, and weaknesses, so too will your bosses.

They're only human after all.

The following is a list of the kinds of bosses you may run into one day. These boss categories are from Monster.com (see the link at the end of the list for more on the types of bosses). As you read the various types, you'll learn something new and probably chuckle a time or two as well, because we all have people in our lives that fit into these categories:

1. The Martyr Boss. The martyr boss is the guy who walked uphill both ways in the snow to school. Everything he does is for the "good of the company." He also walked to and from work for five weeks after his car accident, with both legs broken. How do you compete? You don't. You listen.

2. The Screamer Boss. The screamer boss seems to think that he will get his way if he raises his voice to an unconscionable level—the higher the volume, the higher the commitment. When you boil it down, screamers just want to know that they're being heard, and they want recognition.

3. The Manipulator Boss. This type is extremely intelligent and one of the most dangerous. The manipulator boss is highly focused, very motivated, and always has a secret plan. He looks at people as a means to an end. Your best bet is to be open and honest with him. Your boss, who has long forgotten what truth is, will be left impressed by it.

4. The Bumbling Boss. The bumbler boss is the dunce of the bosses. The best way to deal with your bumbler boss is to help get him promoted. When bumblers are promoted, they are notorious for promoting the people underneath them.

5. The Fearmonger Boss. People do what a "fearsome" boss says because they're afraid of him. He always has a threat, and he constantly follows through with that threat in order to keep his employees acquiescent. This boss has a high turnover to keep up the fear factor, and good employees leave him, refusing to work for such an ogre. Eventually, he will burn out every good employee, and a company's bottom line cannot sustain the costs involved.

6. The Clueless Boss. The clueless boss is not dumb; he's just uneducated. A clueless boss can be a good boss who is just off-track at the moment. The best way to deal with this type of boss is to teach him, and bring him up to speed. You'll be surprised at how fast he comes around, and he'll have you to thank.

7. The Old-School Boss. The old-schooler dwells on the good old days, on "the way things used to be." However, if he is so entrenched in the past, eventually he will stop being able to function in the present. An old-school boss, despite his resistance to move on, does have a great deal of information and can contribute to the best interests of your organization, as long as he is able to accept gradual amounts of change with guidance.

8. The God Complex Boss. The god boss, a true megalomaniac, is about power. You'll notice the engraved gold plate on his office door, desk, and chair proclaiming his rank. He might take outrageous liberties like having an employee clean out his car. When you question him, he'll just point to the gold plates. Rest assured that his cloak of power hides great incompetence. How to get along with a god boss? Humor him. Follow his rules, and create the illusion you're doing things his way.

9. The Teflon Boss. This guy is the king of passing the buck. Any blame slides right off him. He does not give straight answers to straight questions. If something goes wrong, unparalleled documented evidence surfaces to prove he was somewhere else at the time. The non-stick boss is more of a nuisance than a danger. When dealing with him, it's best to keep detailed accounts and records of your conversations.

10. The "What Boss?" Boss. The "What Boss?" boss is always missing in action. He becomes harmless because he's just never there. When he's in the office, take advantage of his presence. You'll feel miffed at the lack of justice—you slaving in your cubicle eight hours a day, five days a week for half his salary, while he's out on the golf course.

11. The Paranoid Boss. The paranoid boss is outright suspicious of everyone's motives. Anything anyone does could be an attempt to undermine him. This boss' feelings of inadequacy will clearly end up interfering in what's best for the company and his employees. What you can do? Reassure him, and always be honest and forthright.

12. The World-on-His-Shoulders Boss. Though this boss might present himself as tough, he can barely hide his inadequacies. He absorbs the world's worries, and worries for the world. He arrives at the office in the morning, flushed and frazzled, because he was lying awake the night before agonizing over numbers and orders. How to deal? Be gentle, but try to avoid much interaction if you can. The nervousness can be contagious.

13. The Buzzword Boss. The buzzword boss loves his designer clothes, cars, pen, and toothbrush. What he loves even more are those clichés he heard at the latest management seminar. Get your barf buckets ready because this boss adores the fact that there's no "I" in team, that he can't spell success without "u," and that for him to assume would make an "ass" out of "u" and "me." Though not for the easily queasy, this boss is essentially harmless.

14. The Buddy Boss. The buddy boss wants to be your friend, not your "superior." He wants you to like him, and because friends stick up for friends, it might be a good investment to spend some time with him. However, be forewarned: hanging out with buddy boss during your work hours could have you working nights to keep up.

15. The Two-Minute Boss. The two-minute boss is a cross between a god boss and a world-on-his-shoulders boss. He impulsively demands control over situations ("What have you done when I was on vacation?") and then cuts off your answer two minutes in because he doesn't have time to discuss it. The two-minute boss constantly gives the impression that he is way too busy to bother with details. Working for this boss is an exercise in the art of speaking concisely.

16. The Patronizing Boss. The patronizing boss is an old-school martyr. Didn't you know? He built the company from the ground up! In fact, he made the chair you're sitting in. You, as an underling, need his holiness's guidance to see you through the most mundane and simple of tasks. His help, however, always leads to—you guessed it—trouble. How to deal with the King of Condescension? Try a little deflation. Ask him how is it that someone as knowledgeable and talented as him is working for this little company.

17. The Idiot Boss. The idiot boss is characterized by cluelessness and stupidity. It's as if he just walked into the office yesterday and started running it. Your choices here can be limited. Doing nothing will leave you embittered, but what can you do when you can't change an idiot? Well, you can change your reaction. The world is full of idiots in charge, but don't let it get you down. Do your personal best, and realize that in some way, your boss serves a purpose. Figure out what it is.

18. Lone Wolf Boss. The lone wolf prefers to ride solo. He stays in his office or works from home, avoiding human contact, especially employee interaction. He could be a tech whiz who was promoted based on his outstanding hard skills, but he's not necessarily a people person. The lone wolf boss leaves you on your own, so don't expect teamwork or career goal discussions. Look to build your work and networking relationships elsewhere.

19. The Perfectionist Boss. The perfectionist is a micro-manager who likes to control all of your work. The behavior is obsessive, and leaves you with very little trust in your own abilities. Over time, you'll learn that nothing you do will ever be good enough for him. Instead of losing all motivation, learn to work for yourself and your own standards. At one point, sit down with your boss and ask him to explain his expectations (even put them in writing) so you both can "get on the same page."

20. The Eccentric Boss. The eccentric boss has unrealistic expectations for his staff. He has a unique way of completing his work, and expects his employees to work in the same manner. He can be gentle, but often causes confusion around his expectations and explanations of projects. This boss is likely to play favorites (as he gravitates towards others with similar interests). The eccentric boss would most likely rather be doing something else, and sometimes this will show.

21. The Great Boss. Ah, the great boss—the supportive motivator—the boss who treats everyone with fairness regardless of politics. He communicates, keeps an open door policy, and encourages others to follow suit. He leads by example, provides superior training, and a positive work environment. He has vision, is not afraid, and doesn't scream. He coaches his staff, and when employees leave, they will talk about him for years to come.

This information was based on the following webpage:

http://hiring.monster.com/hr/hr-best-practices/workforce-management/hr-management-skills/types-of-bosses.aspx

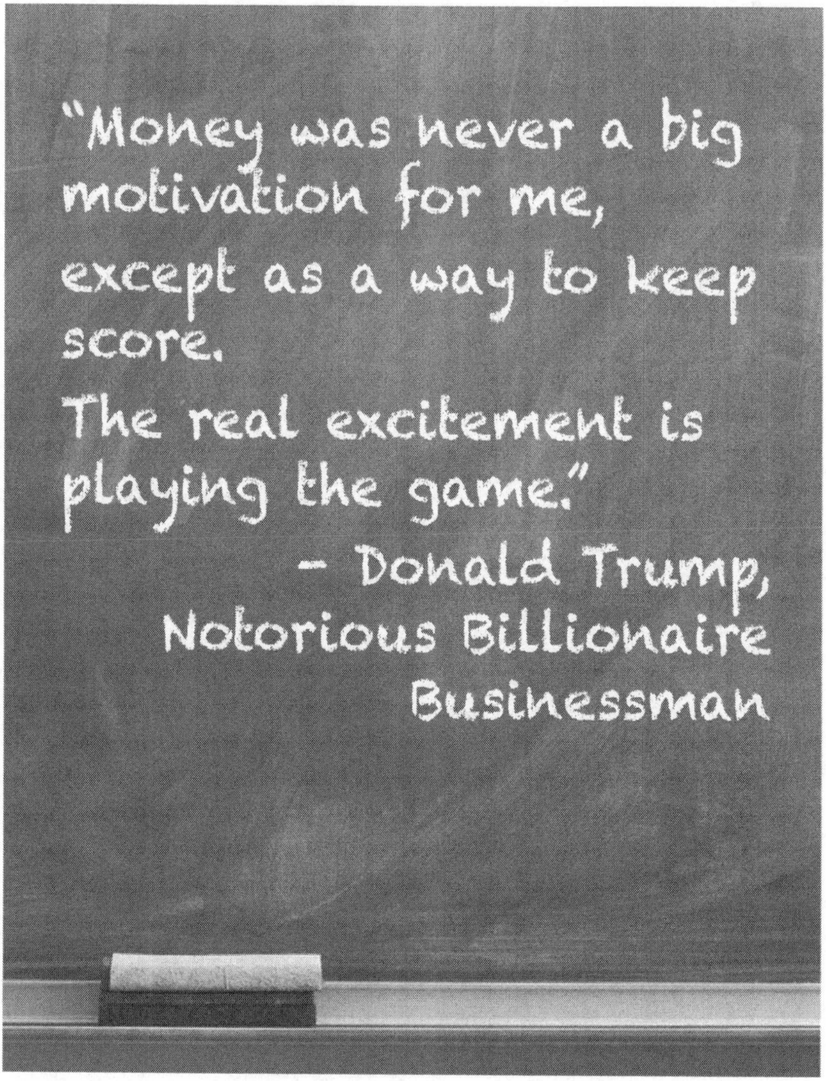
"Money was never a big motivation for me,
except as a way to keep score.
The real excitement is playing the game."
- Donald Trump,
Notorious Billionaire
Businessman

Chapter 12

The Other Players: Your Colleagues and How to Deal With Them

> *"It's your responsibility to sort out the players to figure out who is on your side, who is your competition, and who doesn't really contribute to your success or failure."*
>
> -Stephen Krempl

There is a colorful assortment of players on every sports team. There are the untouchable players, the ones who can do no wrong. There are the momma's boys who love to complain and always find someone to blame when the team loses. Of course, there are the team players that always think of other's contributions before their own. Then there are the star players, the ones who get all the credit for the team's successes no matter how much or little they did. There are the glory hounds; the ones who try to steal the best shots and the spotlight. And then there's the B Team, the second string players, who have to support the better players but don't ever get the glory or the spotlight. They play a major part in the success of the team, but they have to live with the fact that they may never get recognized.

If you've ever played organized sports, you've probably known players like the ones above. You also probably know by now that most of the athletes on your playing field are the competition. But even competitors need allies; and at the end of the day, not everyone on your organization's team will be vying for the same promotions and positions that you want. So, it's your responsibility to sift out the players on your team and figure out who is on your side, who is your competition, and who doesn't really contribute to your success or failure. And the best way to do that is to figure out what role each of them plays.

The Ten Types of Colleagues

Dealing with the wide variety of colleagues in your organization can be tricky terrain—particularly for those who dislike confrontation. The good news is, figuring out which kind of boss or co-worker you're dealing with can be the key to unlocking a solution. The best way to address this is to present ten possible types of colleagues you may face based on sources that include articles from TheSeeker.com and Monster.com, which are websites designed to help jobseekers. The most important thing is not the specific types or variations of personalities you will face, but how you choose to deal with them throughout your career:

1. The Credit Thief. These types of employees love the spotlight and are usually unabashed about taking credit for the success of their co-workers—often to compensate for their own insecurities and shortcomings. When working closely with a credit thief, keep a record of your activities and provide your manager with regular work-in-progress reports. If they try to take credit in your presence, use a "we" statement to assert your involvement.

2. The Office Gossip. Gossips love drama, but their rumor spreading can be damaging to your professional reputation and your career. Avoid engaging in any of their gossip, since anything you say could be held against you. Excuse yourself from negative conversations, or redirect the focus to the task at hand.

3. The Slacker. Slackers often have a knack for doing the bare minimum of actual work, while always appearing to be hard at work or even "worn out" from working. Deal with them by documenting the responsibilities of each team member on the projects you share, ensuring everyone is held accountable for their own workload.

4. The Belittler. Belittlers tear their co-workers down to build themselves up. Don't let them hit your emotional buttons. Standing up for your stances and ideas and calmly refuting their put-downs can stop them in their tracks.

5. The Saboteur. Saboteurs like to make others look bad—and may go out of their way to leave teammates in the lurch. Suggest regular progress meetings with managers to ensure saboteurs can't take advantage of miscommunications or oversights.

6. The Micromanager. Micromanagers can be overly controlling, which can make employees feel undervalued or distrusted. Their fear of losing control may have nothing to do with your performance. The best course of action is to anticipate possible concerns or questions, and provide them with information before they ask. Discuss and get clarification on which decisions require their attention.

7. The Dictator. The dictator's *"my way or the highway"* style of thinking can make it hard to get your ideas heard. Try approaching them in a non-confrontational way, using statements that start with, "Could we…" or "Do you think we might try…"

8. The Coward. Cowards can't take their own stand on any issue, and they lack the willingness or the ability to tell between right and wrong. One day they will hang out with you and another day, they will be seen bonding with your enemy (whatever ruffles the fewest feathers).

9. The Wallflower. This species has a daily fixed routine. They come to work, bury themselves in the office files, take a lunch break, then work more and call it a day in the evening. In short, they mind their own business and have hardly any interest in the world around them.

10. The Bosom Buddy. Despite the presence of all the odd figures at work, there will be one person who you could trust blindly. You may not always find one of these at every organization you work for, but hopefully you will come across a few true friends during your career.[1]

Figuring out which kind of boss or co-worker you're dealing with can be the key to unlocking a solution.

The good news is that these traits usually show up pretty early on in life, so chances are you will probably be able to identify what type of employees many of your college classmates will be, who to partner with, and when its best for you to just steer clear.

Some people aren't worth the drama they cause. And yes, many of these people will be your competition, which means that they will serve as hindrance to your career if you let them. As you read through the list again, start thinking of how you can "flex" your personality when dealing with each type in ways that will make your interactions as efficient and productive as possible.[2]

Six Steps To Resolving Office Conflict

You will have many conflicts throughout your career, both with people vying for the same promotions and recognition you want and with people who you view as allies. The key is to resolve the conflict in a way that allows the relationships—however professional, friendly, or barely cordial they may be—to remain intact, and more importantly, functional and useful. Here are some ways to engage in successful conflict resolution:

1. Always Keep it Together. Stay composed, confident, and professional to show you can deal with conflict with poise. This will also show workplace bullies that you won't be intimidated or sucked in by their behavior.

2. Focus on Solutions. Approach a situation with your boss or colleague with a positive attitude. Focus on solutions rather than finger pointing. Overlook small annoyances and identify the real concern.

3. Think Before You Speak. Think carefully before you speak. When necessary, walk away from a situation and then address the issue later when tempers have settled. This is not a dorm room argument—it's the big leagues, so act the part!

3. Be Professional. Always remain professional. Maintain a calm and reasonable demeanor, keeping your emotions in check. You will need to focus on this before you go into the meeting (and use your 5% switch if needed).

4. Don't Run to the Boss. Try to resolve a conflict with your difficult colleague before taking the issue to management. Initiate an open discussion about your professional relationship, and express a desire to work together more positively.

5. The Last Resort. If there is no resolution, follow your company procedures for registering complaints. If you take an issue to your boss or HR, make sure you've taken steps to deal with the problem internally first. That will be the first thing they will ask you.

Conflict can arise in any work environment, so try not to take issues personally—although you will sometimes find that more difficult than you could imagine. Be proactive and take positive measures to contribute to a good working situation. Even if leaving a toxic work environment is the ultimate answer, remaining professional, and continuing to produce work of a high standard, is vitally important for your continued career development.[3]

Footnotes for Chapter 12:

[1]http://excelle.monster.com/benefits/articles/3613-the-25-species-of-coworkers

[2]Oliver, Vicky. B*ad Bosses, Crazy Coworkers & Other Office Idiots: 201 Smart Ways to Handle the Toughest People Issues*. Naperville: Sourcebooks, 2008.

[3]http://theseeker.seek.com.au/7-types-of-difficult-colleagues-or-bosses

Coach's Corner

Identify the Players on Your Team

Whether you are in an office of hundreds of people in your department or in a smaller, more intimate office environment, you will always find several (or all) of the personalities you learned about in this chapter. And the faster you identify them, the better off you'll be because you will know the absolute best ways to interact with each of them according to their strengths and weaknesses.

It's never too early to start learning these tactics, whether you are a freshman or about to embark on your new career. So, for the purposes of this exercise, think of anyone and everyone you know, including classmates, friends, co-workers, or even friends from high school (if you're new to college). For each behavioral/personality type below, label the person in your life who most closely resembles each title. Then in one sentence, write how their type affects they way they interact in a group setting.

The Credit Thief:

The Office Gossip:

The Slacker:

The Belittler:

The Saboteur:

The Micromanager:

The Dictator:

The Coward:

The Wallflower:

The Bosom Buddy:

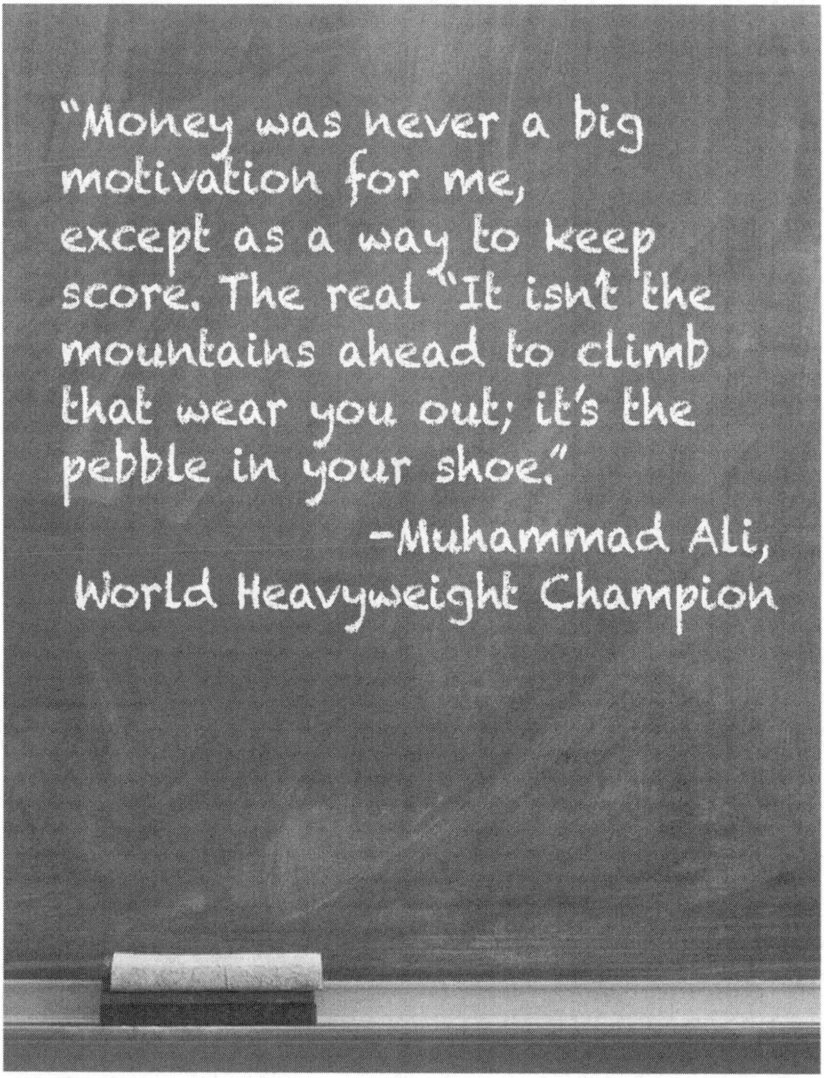
"Money was never a big motivation for me,
except as a way to keep score. The real "It isn't the mountains ahead to climb that wear you out; it's the pebble in your shoe."
-Muhammad Ali,
World Heavyweight Champion

Chapter 13

The Fans: How to Network Internally and Externally to Stand Out

"Nothing you know will make a difference—it is what you use that will make the difference."
-Stephen Krempl

Nothing is more exhilarating for a major league player than when he first steps onto the field and hears the roar of the screaming crowd from the stands. Fans are inspiring and exciting, and they are the reason the teams are out there in the first place. After all, professional sports teams wouldn't even exist without their fans. But fans also provide an added element of pressure. If you lose too many games or misbehave, you can lose their trust and loyalty. And for the die-hard fans, once that loyalty is gone, it's almost always gone for good.

Ultimately when it comes to sports, the end result—the victory—is as much or even more about the fans than it is about the players. And while there are (hopefully) no bleachers next to your desk at work, there are still people who need to be satisfied as a part of what you do. And not just for their sake—

these interested parties greatly affect the bottom line of your organization.

The ways to reach the fans (the people both inside and outside your organization) that you rely on to build your reputation and provide you with advice and ideas is to connect with them in a meaningful, enduring way. That is why the most successful players in the professional world are the ones who have mastered the art and skill of *networking*.

The Four-Step Plan for Building Support

Networking is often thought of as some specific activity or event that you attend, as in "I'm going to a networking lunch," or, "Our company encourages us to join networking groups." But this limited description does a serious disservice to the extent and importance of the word. The definition of *networking* can actually be expanded to include the way you interact with and influence anyone around you who impacts your work in some way. In other words, networking takes place both internally and externally with anyone and everyone who affects the way you do business now and in the future.

"I have many friends that I met networking when I was just starting out. We all have developed our careers over the years and they (some of whom have became big names) are now my supporters, advocates, and friends. My advice is start early."

You need a way to reach the fans out there—the people who make or break your success—because a player is nothing without his or her fans. This chapter will reveal the four steps for building your "fan base" and becoming an influencer with support from within and from outside your organization. Here are the four steps we will briefly cover:

1. The Foundation. Every good plan needs a foundation; and the strongest foundation for building and keeping support is through networking. (This is a lifelong activity.)

2. Strategize and Plan. Next, you have to figure out the best methods and target groups to network with that could build the kind of support system you need to thrive. (This helps focus your limited time.)

3. Execute. The third step is to execute your plan for networking and connecting through establishing rapport. (You hone this skill over time.)

4. Follow-up. The final crucial step is to follow-up. Relationships will wither unless they are maintained. (This is no different than keeping in touch with your friends from college.)

We will spend the most time in this chapter on the foundation—which is networking—so that you will fully understand its critical role in your future career and in the professional world today.

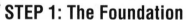

STEP 1: The Foundation

The foundation for support is built on networking. And as I mentioned earlier, networking is not narrowly defined as some specific event you have to attend. Rather, you should network at every opportunity. It's really about finding and building alliances at every level of your organization and outside your organization.

When you act with reciprocity, it will come back to you tenfold in business and your professional life. The most successful professionals out there know that you *give* to *get*—and the very best out there simply *give* to *give*. When you approach your company and private life in this manner, just watch the good that may come your way.

Networking Redefined. So how can you create and use networks to help you get ahead and stand out in business? After all, who has time to "network" when the business of doing our job takes up so much of our valuable time? That's a valid point. It does often seem like there is more *work* than there is *day*. Well, first you have to redefine networking in your mind. If you see it as the unpleasant task of trading favors with strangers, you will not be likely to do it and you will definitely not reap any of its benefits. Networking IS your work and it becomes one of the things you have to *plan* to do. Remember, the earlier you start, the greater the cumulative effect will be down the road.

Unfortunately for many people, they only see the importance of networking after they realized they are out of the loop—not just inside the company, but outside, too—at a moment when their future in the company is at stake.

If you are not interested in becoming a leader in your organization, then perhaps networking is not as important, but if you have plans to transition in to a leadership role, you will reach points in your career that challenge you to rethink both yourself and your role. In the process, you will find that networking—creating a fabric of personal contacts who will provide support, feedback, insight, resources, and information—is simultaneously one of the most obvious and one of the most dreaded developmental challenges that aspiring leaders must address.

The discomfort is understandable, but this is where you switch into your 5% Zone. You need to move beyond your functional group (the function you currently work in) and learn about other issues facing the business. It may be hard to grasp that this will involve relational—not analytical—tasks. Nor is it easy to understand that interactions with a diverse array of current and potential stakeholders are not distractions from your "real work" but are actually at the heart of your aspiring leadership role.

A majority of managers say that they find networking insincere or manipulative and are just an elegant way to use people. That, my friend, is your LV (Little Voice) talking you out of a valuable tool for your career. In his book, *Little Voice Mastery*, Blair Singer describes it like this: "It's the thing inside your head that says, '*What little voice? I don't have a little voice!*' That's the one! We all have one!" And what your LV says to you will determine how far you go in life. [1]

The GREAT leaders all do it and have the widest networks. Not surprisingly, for every leader who constructs and maintains a useful network, there are several who struggle to overcome this inherent resistance and bias to the very idea. Yet the alternative to networking is to *fail*—either in reaching for a leadership position or in succeeding at it. Ultimately, there are two distinct but related forms of networking—Internal and External—and the key to both is your strategic intent.[2]

1. Internal Networking. The purpose of networking internally is to help you manage your current internal responsibilities. It's all about what is going on INSIDE your organization. Make sure you know as many people as you can in your functional area and then spread your net a little further and make sure you get to know people from other functional groups. Volunteering for cross-functional committees and organizing company events are a great start. When it comes to succession planning, the more leaders that recognize you for your good work, the better your chances are for advancement.

2. External Networking. The second form of networking is meant to boost your personal profile and development. It's the kind that you probably think of most often when people talk about networking. But many professionals don't spend enough time on it. Personal networking occurs mostly outside the organization to build up contacts and get referrals. Start by joining the national association for your functional area or local business groups so you can meet others from different companies within your industry. If you are really looking to stand out, then volunteer to join the ex-committee or sub-committee to get to know the leadership of that group. Those may become useful connections later in your career. The other reason you do external networking is to be able to bring in ideas, insights, and benchmark data into your organization from the outside. You will then have access to people from other companies that you have networked with, which greatly increases your credibility within the organization.

3. Thinking About Your Strategic Intent. *Strategic Intent* is all about matching your company's needs with the interest of others. It is perhaps the most game-changing leverage because it opens your eyes to your company's directions and reveals the stakeholders from the outside that you need to enlist to help you with insights. And if you can do this, then you are *really* helping your company.

> Strategic Intent opens your eyes to your company's directions and reveals the stakeholders that you need to enlist to help you with insights.

While most managers and leaders probably pursue both internal and external networking to some degree, your strategic intent is by far the best way to leverage your time and efforts. This is where you strategically network with individuals from companies who may have the same interest on projects, goals, or initiatives that you or your company is working on. For example, if your organization is trying to increase innovation, then finding another company who is on the same path may lead to some insights you had not yet considered.

In order to become a top executive in your organization, to stand out, and to make a difference, networking must become part of your strategic repertoire. Below is a table summary of the two forms of networking, including each one's strategic intent, the main purpose of each, where the networking takes place, who is involved in the process, and the key behaviors you need to display for each to be effective.[3]

The Two Forms of Networking

	INTERNAL	EXTERNAL
STRATEGIC INTENT	Figure out future priorities and get support for the necessary steps to achieve them	Leverage (creating outside-inside links) and Creating Industry Presence
WHY	To increase work effectiveness, maintain and build functional and other links	To enhance personal and professional development while targeting company or personal interests
WHERE	Informal and formal internal meetings and social events.	Industry group talks, functions and conferences. Rotary and Toastmasters club are excellent places. Blogs and chat groups are also good places to start.
WHO	Determined mostly by current tasks and assignments, or volunteering for company wide projects.	Functional seniors or people interested in the areas you and company are focusing on.

STEP 2: Strategize and Plan

The second step toward building relationship and support and expanding your business "fan base" is to strategize. Ultimately your plan should be built on trust and on how dependable you are; but you will find (if you haven't already) that trust is easy to talk about but a little harder to earn. For many, it takes a career to build it, and yet one wrong move can destroy years of effort.

Here is a quick suggestion on how you may approach this subject: First, you must do what you say you will do (that goes a long way). And second, offer assistance or help before asking for something. Here are some other steps you need to consider to use to be most effective for building your strategic networking plan around trust.

1. Have Resolve. Don't be inflexible, but know the commitments you need from co-workers and your networking groups both inside and outside the organization.
2. Do Research. People like to know that you aren't the kind of person who spouts off with nothing to back your words. Do detailed homework and you will impress those around you with your thoroughness.
3. Find Needs. Don't suggest changes or present ideas unless they provide a solution that doesn't just satisfy your own personal needs. Then isolate the need and show how your proposal satisfies the need.
4. Ask for Help. People are more willing to trust and follow those who believe in the power of a team effort. So when it comes time to present ideas or suggest changes, identify whose help you need, and let them know why you need them.
5. Study People. We all want people to acknowledge us for more than who we are on our business card. Take time and learn about a person's operating style to connect with him or her and start to build trust.

The Best Practice More Than the Rest. After you take the steps to build trust as you network and reach out to others, you also have to rehearse. In the same way that you should practice the key things you will say to your new boss within the first few weeks of your new job, you should also rehearse the best ways to network and connect. You can accomplish this most effectively when you:

- Know how to introduce yourself, and include a short description of your project or interest in a succinct sentence.
- Know how your interest fits with the other parties on broader organizational issues.
- Prepare to share what you or the company is doing in an area and know what areas that need to find more information on.

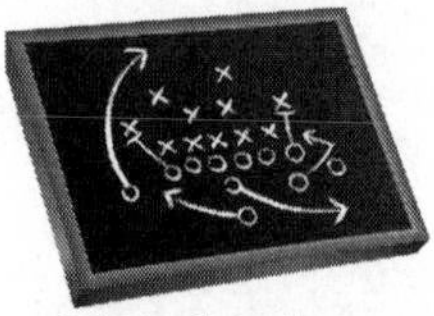

STEP 3: Execute

The third step in the plan to build relationships and support through networking is all about your execution. The most effective way to execute your plan is to have a checklist of things you need to do and ways you will engage with them and *build relationships in a meaningful way*—and you establish rapport through effective communication or using F.O.R.M. When you communicate in an open, honest, and non-defensive way, share your POV, POC, and know your TPV on your area of interest. This all helps builds trust because people will know where you stand, which in turn builds better rapport. Here are some of the most common ways to establish effective lines of communication both inside and outside the organization:

- Find out what the most critical issues are for the person with whom you are networking.
- Demonstrate concern for others' needs first.
- See if it is even appropriate to bring up your identified needs
- If internal, you may need to appeal to the broader department or company goal.
- Gain agreement on a mutual solution to share information or on next steps.[4]

Because we live in such a fast-paced world, many people in business think that the art of rapport building is on its way out. I mean, who has time to stop and consider the needs of everyone else? But if you plan to make your mark and rise in the ranks, I hope you make the time, because doing so will set you apart from the competition. The first step is to decide whom you are going to start networking with. Use the checklist below to determine where and with whom your networking efforts will be most effective.

Internal and External Networking Checklists

INTERNAL NETWORK Function/Dept.	Person	Current Relationship			
		Unsatisfactory		Very Satisfactory	
		1	2	3	4
1.Colleagues/Friends a) Within Department b) Outside Department c) Outside Function					
2. Informal/ Formal Mentors a) Inside Mentors b) Outside Mentors					
3. Access Providers/ Gatekeepers a) Within Department b) Within Function c) Other Depts/Functions 4. Confidant/Coach a) Formal b) Informal					
5. Others					

EXTERNAL NETWORK	Person	Current Relationship			
		Unsatisfactory		Very Satisfactory	
		1	2	3	4
1.Business Friends a) Within Industry b) Other Industries					
2. Professional Advisors (Consultants)					
3. Coaches/Advisors (Role Models, Teachers)					
4. Functional Associations					
5. Professional Development Group(s) Toastmasters, Mastermind Group					

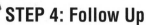

STEP 4: Follow Up

The final phase is another step that often gets tossed to the side because of the breakneck speed of modern business. But when you slow down and take the time to follow up with people, they will remember the extra effort—and they will remember you. Look at follow-up as a way to prepare for a new phase of your career, the phase that will take you to the next level. Here are the things to keep in mind to help you follow-up effectively and in a way that will enhance your reputation and your standing in the business and in the community:

- Establish, meet and monitor the progress of your commitments.
- Keep other people's goals in mind and send useful information their way.
- Keep track of work anniversaries, birthdays and significant events (LinkedIn or such tools should keep you on track).
- Make sure you "calendarize" your next meeting/contact to strengthen relationships.

Ultimately, a good networker and influencer needs three characteristics: 1) Flexibility of behavior to elicit the most useful responses and to help you build trust 2) The ability to notice a person's response and what it means and 3) The good judgement to know whether a response is helpful for the situation.

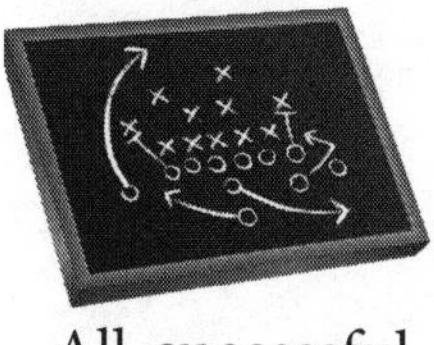

How to Build Better Business Relationships

All successful professionals, regardless of their industry, have one thing in common: They know how to build and maintain relationships. The truth is that some people get caught up in the details of their "job descriptions" and stop recognizing how critical it is to build relationships not only with your internal and external network, but also with vendors, customers, and even your competitors (when appropriate). Here are some tips on how to build stronger business relationships that will last: [5]

- **Ask for Feedback**. An open, honest relationship demands clear communication and encourages constructive input. Suggest helpful ways for others to improve and be open enough to accepting suggestions from others.

- **Listen (More Than You Talk)**. Being a good listener actually highlights your virtues much better than being a big talker does. What sets the "greats" apart from the rest is the fact that they take the time to listen and really understand their co-workers and customers.

- **Make A Routine**. Develop a contact system to ensure that not too much time passes before you reconnect with people. With the widespread use of social media such as Facebook, LinkedIn, and Twitter, it's never been easier to keep in touch.

> When you take the time to follow up with people, they will remember the extra effort—and they will remember you.

- **Be Honest**. If you don't know the answer to a question, say so. People will appreciate your honesty, and that will lay the foundation for a great relationship.

- **Take Notes**. Keep detailed notes on everyone you meet, and then enter those notes into a database. Small details are too important to trust them exclusively to your memory.

- **Be Spontaneous**. From time to time, reach out to someone when there is nothing to gain other than saying hello and checking in. People really appreciate it when they realize that you're looking out for them and not wanting something all the time.

- **Be Proactive.** Using your knowledge of your relationships, forward useful links, articles, and other information that might be of interest to your contacts. It won't take much time and it shows you were thinking about them.

• **Be Real**. Don't be afraid to be vulnerable from time to time. Letting people see the real you builds trust and respect.

• **Turn Mistakes into Opportunities**. Admitting mistakes and correcting missteps will take you far when it comes to building relationships. Many times people just want to hear "I'm sorry" and know that you have a plan for getting back on track.

• **Make it Personal**. Sometimes it is good to send an actual physical letter or card of appreciation as opposed to an email. You can really never say "thank you" enough to clients, customers, colleagues and vendors.

• **Meet Face-to-Face**. Invite your contacts to an event such as sporting event or concert that you would both enjoy, which may deepen the relationship and your connection.

You can attend networking meetings and ask for others' input until you are blue in the face, but if you don't have the ability to understand the responses and feedback you receive, it will all be of little use to you. That is why you must always listen and seek to understand and perhaps more importantly accept that other people have a right to their own reactions and interpretations. When you begin to listen to the suggestions of others, only then will you begin to grasp the full power of your internal and external "fans" out there.

Chapter 13 Footnotes:

[1]Singer, Blair. *Little Voice Mastery: How to Win the War Between Your Ears in 30 Seconds or Less and Have an Extraordinary Life!* Englewood: XCEL Press, 2013.

[2]Sweeney, Joe. *Networking is a Contact Sport: How Staying Connected and Serving Others Will Help You Grow Your Business, Expand Your Influence—or Even Land Your Next Job.* Dallas: BenBella Books, 2011.

[3]http://hbr.org/2007/01/how-leaders-create-and-use-networks/ar/1\

[4]Fuchs, Sidney. *Get Off The Bench: Unleashing The Power of Strategic Networking Through Relationships*. Charleston: Advantage Media Group, 2012.

[5]http://www.inc.com/guides/201101/how-to-build-better-business-relationships.html

Coach's Corner

Trust is a Powerful Instrument

Have you ever trusted someone completely, only to be let down? Most of us have at some point or maybe points in our lives. There is nothing more deflating than the feeling that someone has let you down, abused your friendship, or betrayed your trust.

That one little word—TRUST—can make or break your career the same way that it can make or break the careers of sports stars. People don't want to support players or teams they can't trust. *So, how trustworthy are you?*

Name one time when you lost someone's trust and what you did to lose it.

If you tried to gain the person's trust back, how long did it take, what was required, and were you successful?

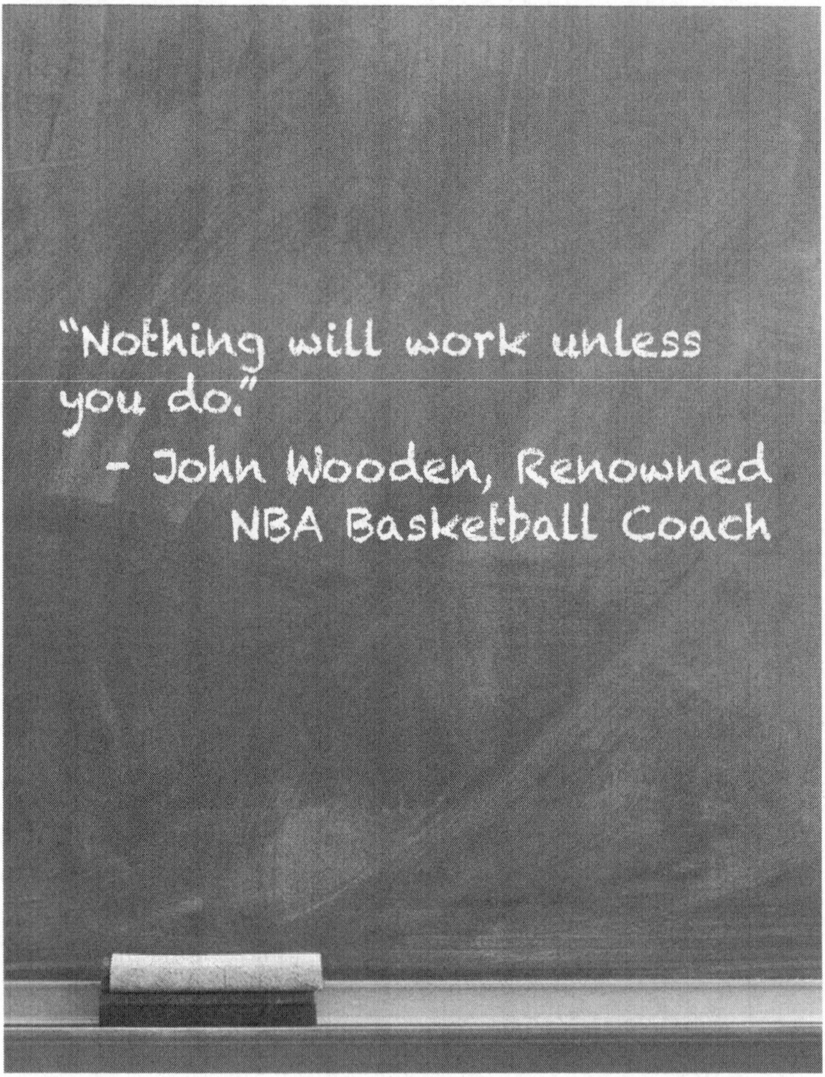
"Nothing will work unless you do."
- John Wooden, Renowned NBA Basketball Coach

Chapter 14

The Ninety-Day Game Plan: Your Checklist For Success

"You're hired... So it's time to show everyone that you know what to do."

-Stephen Krempl

Welcome to the Real World! You prepared, you studied, you chose a great major, you found the company where you want to begin your exciting new career, and even better, you got the job!

Now it's time to answer the question: "You're Hired! Now What Do You Do?"

Every rookie needs a game plan. From the moment that a new recruit gets scouted and selected by the coaches, the clock starts ticking. Every interaction he has with players and coaches and every action that he takes both on and off the field all work to form the first impression that the team and the fans have of him and his future on the team.

What kind of impression do you want to make? It's completely up to you—and if you want it to be a good one, then you need a plan to get there. This final chapter will give you a solid framework to stand out and get noticed in the first ninety days of your new career.

I've broken the ninety-day period into three phases. Obviously, the time periods and some of the activities themselves are flexible, which means that you will probably perform a few of the activities in more than one of the phases. This is simply a general framework to get you started in the right direction. Here is a summary of the three phases and why each is critical to your success:

PHASE I (Day 1-30): Be Quick Off the Blocks

"Welcome to the team. Now what was your name again?" Early in phase I, no one knows you yet. You've only met your boss at this point (and that was probably a brief encounter during one of the interview stages). You will be getting introduced to and getting to know your team members. They don't know you very well yet and may have only heard your name mentioned. In fact, as is the case with most rookies, they will be skeptical of you until they see how you perform. The first phase includes activities that you need to engage in from the time you receive your acceptance letter all the way through the first month on the job. During this phase, it's your goal to be "quick off the blocks" and get ahead as soon as you can. This is the make-or-break phase that will begin to form the first impression your team and your boss have of you for years to come.

PHASE II (Day 31-60): Become a Starting Player

"Nice play out there, kid. Good hustle." In phase II, you have already started to make a name for yourself. The buzz about you is positive. Other team members have started to trust you with a few tasks. But your work has just begun. You've shown that you've got hustle and that you have the potential to be a starter, but you've got a long way to go before you solidify your place on the team. These activities will help you build rapport and show the team that you are a perfect fit and are ready to contribute and win.

PHASE III: (Day 61-90): Solidify Your MVP Status

"Keep this up and you'll be player of the year." In the third phase, you are rocking it at your new job. A few months in, and you can tell that your boss feels excited to have you on his team. You show that you know your stuff, you're teachable, you are ambitious, and you are a team player. Now it's time to step up to the plate and hit it out of the park. The activities in phase III include the details that will further set you apart and show that you take a winning approach to everything you do.

Below is the Action Plan for your first ninety days. Use this plan as a checklist—and know that once you check off every box you will already be on your way to having the kind of superstar career you deserve!

THE NINETY-DAY GAME PLAN

PHASE I (Day 1-30)
Be Quick Off the Blocks

☐ **Write a Letter.** Write a letter to yourself that you will read one year from now. In the letter, tell yourself where you want to be. Include details such as how much overtime you are willing to work, what you want your standing with the boss to be, any promotions or jobs you are targeting on the horizon, and the kinds of relationships you want to have with your colleagues.

☐ **Know Your Why**. Your new company that will be the place you spend the majority of your time over the next few months or years. Remind yourself why you chose it in the first place.

☐ **Do Your Homework.** Just because you have the job doesn't mean your research is done. Read articles about your company and find out as much as you can about their culture and their history. Know the most common accolades they receive as well as any problems with the company. It's useful for the future—because *knowledge* is both power and leverage.

☐ **Find Stories.** As you start out remember to gather stories that will show how much you fit in. Remember the more stories you have from different sources, the more people will think you have been around a while.

☐ **Say Thanks.** Make sure you send a personal thank you card letting your boss know how much you appreciate him choosing you. Also, thank your recruiter that placed you if you used one. Consider sending a gift card to someone who helped you get the job. (Be sure to send it to their work address.) Let them know you are excited to come on board and why.

☐ **Dress to Impress.** Make sure your wardrobe is up to par and appropriate for the company you joined. Get a nice belt, nice shoes, a few suits, and some basics that will make you look sharp. The little details are important. And of course, couple this with excellent hygiene (which includes shaving for the guys and professional hair for the girls).

☐ **Be Proactive.** Is it possible to get your business cards early? You should inquire how you could order them ahead of time so that you can, have them on day one. Figure out what "busy work" and other paperwork you can get done ahead of time before your first day even arrives. No one else in orientation will do this, so it will make you look clever and ambitious.

☐ **Know Your Route.** It may sound obvious, but you can't be late your first day. Take a practice run and learn exactly how you are going to get to work. And be sure to take that practice run during rush hour! Simulate the exact conditions you will have on your first workday.

☐ **Get Tech Ready.** Is your tech up to date? Do you have the right smartphone for your company or will they issue you one (some prefer that all employees use a Blackberry, Android, etc)? Also, figure out what tech you will need to be relevant and even find out what CRM systems or other systems they use. You can lessen your learning curve and be ahead of the class if you know a little about the system beforehand.

☐ **Read the Manual.** Many times a company provides the employee training manual before orientation. Read the entire employee/training manual before your first day if you can. Don't let orientation be the first time you hear all the info.

☐ **Prepare Questions.** Make sure you've got good questions for orientation day. You can stand out on the first day and avoid being another bump on a log. Say something that will differentiate yourself like, "If I need to work late, are there any special procedures in place or rules about this?"

☐ **Get the Goods**. Find out all the "stuff" you need and get as much of it as you can (and as soon as you can) such as any necessary licenses, parking passes, or clearance badges.

☐ **Remove Your Resume**. Take your resume off the career and job sites! It just looks bad. And if your boss sees it, he will wonder why it's still out there.

☐ **Get LinkedIn.** Update your LinkedIn profile with your new job title and start linking with your bosses and supervisors right away. And put a good profile picture on there (not a photo from the last keg party you attended in college)!

☐ **Clear Your Calendar**. Make sure you haven't planned any vacations right after you start. There are probably going to be some things (vacations, parties) you can't attend that you used to be able to. Even if you get two weeks of vacation, there are certain busy times for each organization. So find out when those times are and plan accordingly. Remember you often don't start accruing vacation days after six months, so check your company policy.

☐ **Start 5% Zone Prep**. Starting Identifying your 5% situations. What meetings are going to be the most important in the next few months? Which times will your CEO or the VP of your department be present to meet you and hear your questions and suggestions?

☐ **Find Their Biggest Problems**. Remember to find out the biggest problems of your boss, function, or company so you can find ways to help solve or work towards solving them.

☐ **Be Prepared for Meetings**: Don't forget to prepare your POV for meetings, and if you get a chance to include TPV, please make sure you do.

PHASE II (Day 31-60)
Become a Starting Player

☐ **Determine the Roles**. Figure out the roles that each of your team members plays, as well as your boss. Use the types and roles you read about in this book to determine the roles that are present in your workplace. When you ID the players, you can then figure out the best partners and allies.

☐ **Get to Know the Boss.** Find out your boss's preferred communication style and the expectations on responding to requests. What does he or she absolutely dislike?

☐ **Find your Place**. Now that you have been on the job for a month or two, you can fully assess where you are going to provide the most value. So decide that role YOU are going to play and what you'll be known for. Are you going to be the guy everyone comes to for PowerPoint help? Are you going to be the person everyone trusts with secrets? Are you the go-to guy for creative ideas? Determine what role you want to play and then get really good at it.

☐ **Decorate Your Space**. If you haven't already done so, bring some personal touches to the office to soften up your space. Make it look like you've been there for years. The best place to get company paraphernalia is to look around when people leave or move offices and leave stuff behind. I call this strategic scrounging.

☐ **Be Early to Work**. When you are new (and even if everyone else is always late) you should be early. It tells people that you can be trusted and that you are reliable.

☐ **Brown Bag It?** At this point you know whether everyone brings their lunch or goes out to lunch. It may be tempting to go out to lunch every day, but consider the money it costs to eat out every day. But then also consider that bringing your lunch may save you money, but also it may ostracize you from the group. In other words, become more aware of the little things and the subtle politics and do your best to fit into the culture. Remember pay attention!

☐ **Story Collection.** Continue collecting stories. Pay attention at lunch as colleagues are sharing "war stories" and other things about the company. Store them all away (because you never know when you'll need them).

☐ **Get Their Digits.** As early as possible, get the phone numbers and email addresses for the important supervisors in the company (maybe not the big boss, but if possible and permissible, then him or her as well). If you have a question in the first month or two, it's nice to be able to reach out to the right people (and it shows initiative).

❑ **Find the Right Buddy.** During orientation, you probably made some friends. Now it's time to assess your early friendships and establish the best work buddies. Don't try to jump rank too early, but rather find that other person who joined around the same time you did and who is ambitious, and align yourself with him or her. Don't yoke yourself with anyone who is lazy or negative, because people will categorize you by the company you keep.

❑ **Skip the Drama**. Don't bring any personal drama into your workplace. If you have an argument with your girlfriend or boyfriend, keep it to yourself. You are too new to ever mention personal life drama. Really, no one should bring that stuff to work, but the veterans might be able to get away with it. You? Not yet.

❑ **Start a Log**. Keep a log of projects you have worked on and the things you have done. The next time a performance review comes up or you are up for a promotion, you can bring up specific, actionable things you accomplished. You can't rely on your memory for all of that stuff, so start writing it all down. It will become an invaluable resource down the road.

❑ **Read (Lots of) Books**. Read and then read some more. Read about business and about leadership. The more you read, the faster you will assimilate. A great place to start is by subscribing to Executive Summaries, which are six- to eight-page condensed book summaries.

❑ **Talk the Talk**. Learn business talk and then practice talking and receiving business talk. Communication is brief in business. It's not anything like college where the pace was more laid back. People can sound rude when they are really just in a hurry. Learn to get past this and thicken your skin so you don't take it personally.

☐ **Mentor and Coach**. Start the process of identifying either an internal or external coach or mentor who can help be a sounding board to you at the start of your career.

☐ **Start Using Your 5% Zone**. Start really using those 5% situations. And now is the perfect time because you now know what kinds of contributions other employees make during meetings—so you can figure out how to add value to meetings in ways that no one else is using!

PHASE III: (Day 61-90)
Solidify Your MVP Status

☐ **Get More Stories**. Collect story after story. By now you have good rapport with your team. Find out why they like the company and get specific stories that reinforce your understanding of the culture and the business.

☐ **Assess Your Reputation**. What are you going to be known for? Have you figured it out yet? I hope so. By month four and beyond, your reputation is fairly set with your team, so make sure you continue to reinforce your good standing.

☐ **Remember Your Place**. It may be tempting at this point to loosen up a bit. But you still haven't earned the right to act the way that others who have been there for ten years act. When you establish the ground rules for behavior after hours and at meetings, then make sure you still err on the side of extra caution. (You're still new.)

☐ **Ask for Feedback**. Ask the boss to provide you with feedback on how you can improve, and encourage him to give you constructive criticism as well. No one ever asks what he or she needs to improve. Show how teachable and ambitious you are by inviting the feedback and then USE the suggestions your boss provides without taking it personally.

☐ **Treat Everyone with Respect**. You never know who's watching and who is connected to whom. Be kind and considerate to the janitor, to the delivery guy, and to the IT assistant. Your kindness will be remembered and it will be noticed.

☐ **Ask For More Work**. Go ask your boss or supervisor for more responsibility. Tell him you are willing to work on other projects (if you decide you have the time).

☐ **Reveal a New Skill**. Remind your boss of a skill you bring to the table that is not being utilized. For example, you can say, "I didn't know if you knew this, but I speak fluent Spanish. Would that be useful to the company in some way?"

☐ **Stay Organized**. Keep an organized area and be clean, electronically as well. Develop your own system for keeping everything in tiptop shape. No supervisor wants to see you fumbling on your computer as you search for the right file.

☐ **Get the Coffee**. Sometimes the small stuff can be huge. Make a point to get to work early and make the coffee once or twice a week. Remember the little things. Wash your dishes. Refill the water jug. Don't drink the last cup of coffee. And whatever you do, don't eat anyone else's food out of the communal fridge! Your team and your boss will notice all of these things.

☐ **Avoid Gossip (Like the Plague).** As tempting as it is by this phase, do not get caught up in office gossip. There are no such things as secrets in corporate America.

☐ **Remind Yourself Why**. Be aware of the specific values you add to the company. At any given moment do a self-check and ask yourself what you bring to the table. Why are you here and why are you indispensable to the company? Be ready for that question at all times!

☐ **Learn the Rhythms**. Know the natural rhythm and cycle of your business. If you know that the earnings report comes out at the end of every quarter, you know that's probably not the time to go in and ask for something that would require a large portion of the budget. Understand your company's business cycle and it will help you understand moods, such as when your boss will be more aloof, intense, and times when you should lay low. Then find the lulls when it's better to approach him with something unpleasant.

☐ **Make External Associations**. Identify and join your functional or industry association. Start attending meetings and begin the process of networking early in your career.

☐ **Get to Know Your Boss**. Find out things about your boss's non-work activities when possible such as hobbies, favorite sports teams, and alma mater.

A Final Word of Advice

Maybe you are a freshman or just starting out your senior year and you aren't quite ready for the Ninety-Day Game Plan yet. Well, you need a plan, too. In order to help you stay focused on your goals and get to the finish line (landing your first job in the real world), go to **www.WinningintheWorkWorld.com** to download your FREE planning worksheets today. They will provide you with a way to write down some of your goals and help keep you accountable for reaching them. And remember to use the **COACH'S CORNER** exercises again and again as you progress through college to reinforce the material, give you the practice you need to stand out, and keep you on track.

These are the skills no one else is learning.

These are the actions that will set you apart.

These are the steps for becoming an all-star.

Congratulations on making the choice to stand out and to win at any job in absolutely any industry! If you use even a few of the techniques from this playbook, there will be no stopping you or your career. Because let's face it—even though the competition may be global and it may be cutthroat, you know you bring a lot to the table. And with the right moves, everyone else will know it, too. So start solidifying your place as a starter, as a winner, and as a champion in your company from the moment you step into the office.

If you don't achieve results in an organization, then why are you there? This is not only the truth; it's also what your boss and others on your team will be thinking when they see someone who is not taking the time to add value, be different, be proactive, and stand out.

We should all be striving to produce results. However, if you achieve results but no one likes you in the process, that's also fatal. It will come back to haunt you someday, and that's when you'll discover that you can't get very far when you don't stop and take the time to connect with those around you.

To move up in the organization, you must have what many call "people skills" and an "EQ" (Emotional Quotient). With these two skill sets, you can get along with almost anyone and make others around you feel comfortable. You also need to make sure you get honest feedback on how you are really doing (instead of "Wow you are so great" as they talk about you behind your back). Ask your supervisor or someone in Human Resources. The point is to get feedback—otherwise how will you improve? In the sports world, players and coaches know that the best way an athlete or team can improve is to get constant coaching feedback and then adjust their practice accordingly.

Don't get disheartened if your style does not work in your first organization. Many times, your style will work better in one place over another. That's why in sports some players will dramatically improve just by switching teams. It is fascinating how a change of team or supervisor changes everything when it comes down to a simple culture or style mismatch. Of course, if your style does not work in your first three places, you might need to question what you are doing wrong.

Your time is valuable, and so I thank you for spending some of your time here. I now gladly send you on your way into the world where opportunities abound. I trust you will make the right calls, study the plays, and practice the right skills.

And when you do, you will become the MVP.

For More Work World Wisdom :-

www.WinningintheWorkWorld.com

Winning in the Work World

After several years and thousands of dollars spent on your college education, are you truly ready to excel in the work world?

Keep looking-you won't find any classes called "How to Quickly Climb the Corporate Ladder" listed in the any school curriculum guides. The fact is that college is simply not designed to teach you how to make a strong impression in the early stages of your career

Winning in the Work World is the pioneering comprehensive program designed to help students and recent graduates understand what leaders are really looking for so they can choose to have a powerful head start to a rewarding and meaningful career.

1. The Six-Module Online Series "Get Ready for the Work World" Includes: Powerful rules to build your standout career by Choosing a winning approach to your first job Learning the written and unwritten rules for achieving success Discovering and mastering complex office scenarios you may encounter Building networks internally and externally in order to stand out

2. The Key Functional Questions Manual Will Provide: Important questions to answer about the primary functional disciplines What you need to know to look well sharp and well prepared A reference manual that instructs you on how to stand out from your peers

3.A Three-Phase Checklist for the First 90 Days Will Enable You To: Take the information from the book and the guide and make it your own Customize the tips and strategies to fit your specific career Continually remind yourself what it takes to stand out so that excellence becomes a personal habit.

4. Dynamic Interviews with Corporate Executives Will Equip You With: Insider secrets from executives on what they are looking for from their new job entrants The ability to listen and learn directly from the masters of the corporate world The reasons why they have enjoyed such successful careers An inside look of what they are looking for from future executives like you!

Your Career ead start cannot wait!
Start "Winning in the Work World" today.
Access the program that gives you a
jumpstart to your career at:
www.WinningintheWorkWorld.com

Who is Stephen Krempl?

Stephen Krempl is a speaker, author, and trainer who has helped global leaders and students alike get noticed in an increasingly global marketplace. As CEO of Krempl Communications International, he and his team researched and developed a series of interventions that assist individuals and organizations develop a Global Executive Mindset (G.E.M.) through workshops, coaching, and assessments. He is now spreading the G.E.M. message to universities, enabling students to better prepare for their entry into the corporate world.

Over the last twenty+ years, Stephen has worked for *Fortune 500* companies such as Starbucks, Yum! Brands, PepsiCo, and Motorola. As CLO for both Starbucks and Yum! Brands, he assisted in developing their learning and organizational strategies and built capabilities for both franchisees and suppliers. Stephen currently assists his international clients to help develop curriculum, facilitate high level team meetings, and obtain accreditation for their internal programs. He enjoys speaking and writing books and is frequently asked to speak at conferences.